PRAISE

MENTOR to MILLIONS

"Failure is not fatal. We can choose to stand on top of our pile of failures or be buried by them. In *Mentor to Millions*, Mark Timm and Kevin Harrington . . . show us the mind-set, focus, and action plan we need to turn personal and professional failure into exponential success."
— Dave Ramsey, best-selling author and radio host

"Kevin Harrington gives you the curiosity and tools you need to find new solutions, get your ideas to market, and learn how to scale and build lasting relationships. *Mentor to Millions* is like having Kevin as your personal mentor!"
— Barbara Corcoran, businesswoman and Shark from *Shark Tank*

"A powerful resource. Let Mark Timm and Kevin Harrington equip you to leverage mentoring and focus so you can regain your work-life balance and experience the life you desire."
— Michael Hyatt, *New York Times* and
Wall Street Journal best-selling author

"If you want to know the lessons and formulas Kevin and Mark have learned over the past 30 years . . . read this book."
— Joe Polish, founder of Genius Network

"Undeniably powerful, insightful, and vulnerable approach to doing life and business. A must-read!"
— Dan Sullivan, Strategic Coach

"Put your seat belt on and get ready for an incredible ride. . . . Inspiring, grounded, and immeasurably practical. Don't miss out on Kevin and Mark's life-changing message."
— Les Parrott, Ph.D., #1 *New York Times* best-selling author and founder of BetterLove.com

"There is a secret formula behind why Kevin Harrington has become one of the most successful entrepreneurs today. In this book, Mark and Kevin have put this formula into a framework that shows high levels of success are attainable for anyone."
— Roland Frasier, Principal, DigitalMarketer.com, Scalable.co, All Channels Media, LLC

"In *Mentor to Millions*, Mark and Kevin lay out a simple but amazingly effective blueprint so you can duplicate the successes they both enjoy."
— Ray Edwards, communications specialist, marketer, author, and copywriter

MENTOR
to
MILLIONS

ALSO BY

KEVIN HARRINGTON

Act Now! (with William L. Simon)

Key Person of Influence (with Daniel Priestley)

The 100 Best Spare-Time Business Opportunities Today
(with Mark N. Cohen)

Put a Shark in Your Tank

MENTOR
to
MILLIONS

SECRETS OF SUCCESS IN BUSINESS, RELATIONSHIPS, AND BEYOND

KEVIN HARRINGTON AND MARK TIMM

HAY HOUSE, INC.
Carlsbad, California • New York City
London • Sydney • New Delhi

Published in the United States by: Hay House, Inc.: www.hayhouse
.com® • *Published in Australia by:* Hay House Australia Pty. Ltd.: www
.hayhouse.com.au • *Published in the United Kingdom by:* Hay House
UK, Ltd.: www.hayhouse.co.uk • *Published in India by:* Hay House Publishers India: www.hayhouse.co.in

Cover design: Chris Davis, Madstacc Creative
Interior design: Julie Davison
Indexer: Joan Shapiro

Library of Congress has cataloged the earlier edition as follows:

Names: Harrington, Kevin, author. | Timm, Mark, author.
Title: Mentor to millions : secrets of success in business,
    relationships, and beyond / Kevin Harrington and Mark Timm.
Description: 1st edition. | Carlsbad, California : Hay House, Inc., [2020
CCN 2020025895 | ISBN 9781401959104 (hardback) | ISBN
    9781401959111 (ebook)
Subjects: LCSH: Success in business. | Entrepreneurship. | Success.
Classification: LCC HF5386 .H2675 2020 | DDC 658.4/09--dc23
LC record available at https://lccn.loc.gov/2020025895

Tradepaper ISBN: 978-1-4019-7061-1
E-book ISBN: 978-1-4019-5911-1
Audiobook ISBN: 978-1-4019-5916-6

10 9 8 7 6 5 4 3 2 1
1st edition, September 2020
2nd edition, November 2022

SUSTAINABLE
FORESTRY
INITIATIVE
Certified Chain of Custody
Promoting Sustainable Forestry
www.sfiprogram.org
SFI-01268

SFI label applies to the text stock

Printed in the United States of America

I'd like to dedicate this book to my father, Charlie. He was my first mentor and shaped my entrepreneurial spirit. I hope I can be as good a mentor to other entrepreneurs as he was to me, and if I'm lucky, this book will share some of his wisdom with you, the reader.
— Kevin Harrington

I would like to dedicate this book to Zig Ziglar, the great motivator and disrupter. I was blessed to be mentored by Zig Ziglar at an early age and it changed the trajectory of my life. That relationship led me to constantly seek mentors in my life, and to be a mentor to others. Some decades later I met Kevin Harrington for the first time through Zig's children, Tom, Julie, and Cindy, which directly led to this book. Zig's famous quote, "You can have everything in life you want, if you will help enough other people get what they want," was the foundation of our mentorship relationship and forged the writing of this very book. May this book serve as your motivation to become a mentor to others or to find the right mentor for your life—or both— because such a relationship is truly priceless.
— Mark Timm

CONTENTS

Foreword .... **xi**

Prologue .... **xv**

Chapter One: **1**
But . . . Why Kevin?

Chapter Two: **17**
Get the Right Mind-Set

Chapter Three: **35**
Aggressive Curiosity

Chapter Four: **51**
Get Focused and Make a Plan

Chapter Five: **67**
Take Action

Chapter Six: **83**
From Failure to Phoenix

Chapter Seven: **97**
Multiply Your Efforts

Chapter Eight: **111**
Build Your Dream Team

Chapter Nine: **125**
Get Scale (in Everything)

Chapter Ten: **141**
To Babson and Back Again

Epilogue: **153**
"We Have to Be Timms"

Free Resources for Your Success **161**

But Wait, There's More! **163**

Index **167**

Acknowledgments **173**

About the Authors **179**

FOREWORD

Much More Than That

This is not just another book on entrepreneurial success. It's much more than that.

If you want to learn how Kevin Harrington started more than 20 businesses that each exceeded 100 *million* in sales, then this is a good book for you.

But this book is much more than that.

If you want a simple way to approach your business with specific mind-sets and action steps that will lead you to entrepreneurial success, then this is a good book for you.

But this book is much more than that.

This book is about much more than just being financially successful.

My father once said, "Money will buy you a bed, but not a good night's sleep; a house, but not a home; a companion, but not a friend."

Mentor to Millions has woven through its core the reason why we want a successful business in the first place—to enhance and add to the relationships we cherish most: the relationships we have with our family, our friends, our partners, and those we serve through our business.

When we first dream about starting our businesses, we imagine all of the successes we will have. Those thoughts get our blood flowing and our imagination churning. We develop a vivid "before-and-after" picture in our mind and, with boundless energy, we tackle all of the challenges before us. The hours and days quickly turn into weeks and months. The grind begins and we tell ourselves the relationship costs are part of the "price" of doing business.

STOP. This is a lie. You do not have to suffer damaged, distant, and broken relationships as you create your dream business.

You do, however, have to be more intentional than ever about your relationships. I believe God created us for relationships, and a business done right revolves around the relationships in our life—not the other way around.

I'm betting that a number of you reading this right now are struggling to figure this out. You're struggling to reconcile the idea that your relationships don't have to suffer for your business, and vice versa. Chance are you're in the thick of it and doing the best you can—and that's okay.

Because this book will show you that you're not alone.

Mark Timm lives a life most entrepreneurs only dream about—but he didn't come by it easily. He reached a moment in his life where he realized that all of his successes came at the cost of deep interpersonal relationships with his wife and children.

Instead of accepting that the hustle and grind was the way things had to be, he decided to make a change. No longer would he make a choice between business and family. He would do the right thing. He would become the right kind of entrepreneur.

One invested in the business of family.

The story that follows will teach you how to be successful in business, to be sure. But embedded in those lessons are tales of how Mark learned the true meanings of friendship, love, and hope, learned both directly and indirectly, from one of the world's greatest entrepreneurs—our friend Kevin Harrington.

When I reached the epilogue of *Mentor to Millions*, I can honestly say that few things have ever touched me like that. It was powerful. Beautiful. It even brought me to tears. It is an *epic*-logue! You must resist the temptation to fast-forward to it. Trust me, it will be well worth the wait. Also, be prepared: you may have trouble putting this book down once you start.

Because having the business and the family life you want may seem too good to be true.

I promise you it's not.

Are you ready to become the right *kind* of entrepreneur?

Are you ready to have much more than what you've come to expect?

Then turn the page and let Mark and Kevin show you how.

Tom Ziglar
CEO of Ziglar Inc
Proud son of Zig Ziglar

PROLOGUE

Halfway up my driveway, I realized I didn't want to go home.

I should have wanted to. I'd had the kind of day at work that every entrepreneur dreams of. I'd absolutely crushed it. It was one of those days where I made 100 business decisions, and 99 of them were home runs—one of which was scoring an incredibly big sale. I'd had great meetings, terrific phone calls—everything was humming.

My driveway is about a third of a mile, and turning onto it, there is a little hill, so that until you come to the top of it, no one knows you're in the driveway. As I approached that hill, before anyone in the house could see me, I stopped the car. And I sat.

I stayed there, car idling. I didn't want the euphoria of this incredible day to end. It was a banner day, one where nothing could have gone any better—yet I knew that as soon as I made it to the end of that driveway and walked into my house, I'd be hit with the chaos and confusion of my family.

The euphoria would be gone.

It wasn't their fault. My wife and children didn't understand what I did. My children couldn't even spell *entrepreneur*, let alone comprehend what it was Daddy did all day long. I couldn't share with them the joy I was feeling that day. They simply wouldn't get it. Once I walked in that door, I knew they'd hit me with the craziness that is family, and the charge that I'd felt all day would dissipate in an instant.

What was wrong with me? Filing for bankruptcy and losing your business—that's a reason not to want to go home. That's a reason to sit in the car, trying to figure out how you're going to explain things to your family.

My situation was exactly the opposite—but there I sat.

I felt shame about not wanting to go home. I have a deep inner sense that I was put on this earth to be a dad and a husband far more than I was meant to be a CEO and an entrepreneur. Yet my businesses were getting my first and my best, while my family got my last and my least.

It's so easy to justify those decisions because you tell yourself you're providing for your family—who can argue with that? I traveled all the time and missed games and events because I was building the business. And I was doing it to benefit them.

Still, deep down, I knew that we're all here to do something more than just sell some widgets and make some money. My family and business were competing with each other, pulling each other in opposite directions instead of working together harmoniously.

This wasn't the way it was supposed to be, but I didn't know how to change it.

How could family life be so hard when business was so easy to me? How could I make a hundred decisions at work with confidence and clarity, but the very first decision I had to make at home resulted in bedlam?

How could I justify wanting to stay at work longer because I didn't want the buzz of success to end when I was ignoring the people I cared about the most to do it?

That's when it hit me.

What if I had this whole equation backwards?

What if the most valuable business that I would ever own, operate, or even have the chance to have the privilege of being a part of was not the one that gave me all the wins that day?

What if it was the one I was going home to?

In that moment, my businesses were still my businesses. My home was located in the same place. I still had the same family. I still drove home to them in the same F-150 truck I'd left in that morning. With that question, though, my mind-set shifted in an incredibly powerful way—and it changed everything.

In my driveway, at that moment, *I decided that I would treat my family as a business instead of an obligation or a commitment.*

We would be an actual company with a bottom line and enterprise value. I would take all of the things I was good at in business, and I would apply them to the business of my family. For every note that I took at mastermind sessions and conferences, I would take two notes about how I could apply those principles to our new family venture.

I incorporated my family.

From then on, anything I was doing well in my outside business, we did in the family business. We began to have family meetings on Sunday nights. We have a logo and a mission statement. We have shareholder meetings. My youngest child has the same number of shares in the company as I do.

In my work, we use the DiSC personality profile. I gave it to my entire family to take as well, and believe it or not, it works just as well for families as it does for businesses. It gave my family permission to know that we're different. Our kids simply thought that their siblings were weird—they didn't understand that we're all wired differently.

Even the concepts of marketing applied to our new venture. We ask ourselves, *What does it mean to be a Timm? What does your name mean when you're at school, at church, or with your friends? What do you stand for? What is your equity?* Every family has a bottom line, and it may not be measured in dollars and cents. It's much more likely to be measured in relationships and impact.

Doing all of this gave me the ability to fully embrace this journey of being an entrepreneur. I also got permission from my family to do so. Instead of feeling resistance from them, now I heard, "Dad, go learn some more things to bring back to us. This is cool stuff."

Coincidentally—or perhaps not, depending on your point of view—this is what inspired us to start watching *Shark Tank* together on a regular basis. (In case you're unfamiliar, that's a TV show where aspiring entrepreneurs pitch their business to a panel of five investors—or "sharks"—who decide whether or not to back their companies.) We were now a family business, so what better show to view together than one whose framework is all about business? My 10-year-old daughter, Mary, decided that Kevin Harrington, genius entrepreneur and father of the infomercial, was her favorite shark.

Her fascination with him got me to thinking.

I've always been big on coaching and mentorship. Before my epiphany in the driveway, I wanted to be an entrepreneur only to make a lot of money to bring back to my family. Now I wanted to learn from the best entrepreneurs in the world, not just to be successful, but to take their *knowledge* and apply it back to my family.

Watching Kevin give advice to up-and-coming business owners each week, I asked myself, *Who taught me the most about ideas I can pass on to make our incorporated family a success?*

Then I remembered: Zig Ziglar.

Zig had been a mentor to me as an up-and-coming entrepreneur—really an accidental entrepreneur. I met Zig in person in 1990 in Kansas City, Missouri, at the national FFA (Future Farmers of America). After I spoke with him for a time, he put his hand on my shoulder, looked me in the eyes, and said, "Young man, I believe in you. Will you come to Dallas, Texas, and be my personal guest at my 'Born to Win' conference?" This conference was Zig's high-end training program for CEOs and other executives. Here I was, a literal farm boy raised in "Somewhere," Indiana. I was told to go to school, get a college degree, and get a good, stable job working for someone. I hadn't been raised to be an entrepreneur, and I certainly wasn't taught how to be one. I'd needed Zig to help me have the courage to start my own entrepreneurial journey, as I had no one to guide me. The rest, as they say, is history.

What better way to help build my family "business" than to impart to them the lessons he had passed on to me?

So that's exactly what I did.

I immersed them in Zig's teachings. I taught them about motivation, inspiration, and mind-set, just as he had done for me. My son Markus has now listened to Zig's first speech, "Biscuits, Fleas, and Pump Handles," at least 17 times, to the point where he can practically quote it verbatim.

It was beautiful to watch my children not just embrace Zig's wisdom, but actually integrate it and put it into action. Our little family corporation was coming together, and that gap between my business and family was bridged in a way I could only imagine.

But something was still missing.

I still felt this hole that wasn't being filled by what was happening, and I didn't understand it—at first. Then, as I continued to mentor my children, something clicked. I realized that I didn't have a mentor of my own.

Of course, Zig had taught me things in the past, but it had been mostly around personal motivation and inspiration.

Now here I was, both an entrepreneur and a mentor myself—but still with no present-day, real-time mentor in my life.

And for the first time, I felt the absence. It was like a hole in my life that I hadn't even realized. I had no idea where to go find one. I mean, the only mentor I'd ever had in my life to that point was a mentor from afar, and Zig was long dead.

Where does a grown man find a mentor?

I had no idea how to deal with this, so I sat with it and felt frustrated. Mary and I were watching *Shark Tank* when she noticed.

"Dad, what's wrong?"

I have a strict honesty policy with my children, so I told her. "Well, honey, I was thinking about how I mentor you, but I don't have a mentor. I would like one, but I don't really know where to find one."

"Dad, I know! Why don't you ask Kevin Harrington to be your mentor?"

I laughed. Her enthusiasm was so warm and infectious, but I had no illusions about Kevin Harrington being my mentor—there was no chance.

I explained to her that Kevin had taken more than 20 businesses and generated hundreds of millions in profits. He was the ultimate serial entrepreneur and was in demand all over the world. He certainly wouldn't have time for someone like me.

Mary, though, was not one to give up so quickly.

"But, Dad, Kevin goes on TV to help entrepreneurs just like you! Why wouldn't he help you? I bet he would, you just have to ask. Doesn't Zig Ziglar say you can have anything in life you want if you will just help enough other people get what they want?"

I laughed. The student was already teaching. "Yes, he does say that. Okay, Mary. I'll look into that."

I feel terrible about it now, but I lied to her. I said that knowing that I never would.

And I never did. I'm a risk-taking entrepreneur—but I'm also realistic. I would have to find a mentor somewhere else.

Months later, things were going so well with mentoring my family that I decided to reach out to the Ziglar family to tell them about our little experiment. They immediately fell in love with the concept—so much so that we decided to work on a joint venture together called "Ziglar Family," aimed at helping families go from merely surviving to thriving.

As we worked together and the project found its legs, the CEO of the Ziglar Family called me. He wanted to expand the program and had some ideas on how to do it.

"Mark, these are all great ideas. I also want you to talk to, and possibly work with, one of our company advisors. You might have heard of him. He's pretty well known."

"Oh really?" I said. "Who's that?"

"Kevin Harrington. He's on *Shark Tank*. Do you watch that show?"

I couldn't believe it.

I actually started laughing out loud on the phone. I had to explain to the CEO that I wasn't laughing at the idea—that, in fact, I loved the idea, of course.

I am a religious man, but had I not been, this might have made me believe in God. Because seriously—what were the chances?

Kevin and I had our first phone call and immediately hit it off. The first one led to a number of phone calls, many at my kitchen table with Mary eagerly listening by my side.

Kevin agreed quickly that we'd work together on the Ziglar project, and while that was terrific and exciting, what had become obvious—almost immediately—was that even in the most basic discussions, I was learning more from him than I ever had working on my own as an entrepreneur. He was teaching me, and he didn't even know it.

In the mission of providing mentorship to the business of my family, I had found the mentor and the lessons I had been looking for—and I wanted more. A lot more. Not just of the lessons, but of his time, in order to build more than just a mentor-mentee arrangement. I wanted to develop a relationship built on trust and respect.

Since then, Kevin and I have embarked on many ventures together. In fact, as of the writing of this book, we are involved in 10 different ventures, and it's all because of that first one. Some will yield significantly more return than the first, but we never would have developed this relationship without it. It set the stage for us to realize that we truly enjoy working together, as well as like and respect one another.

It also allowed me to see, firsthand, that Kevin's success was not an accident, and it had nothing to do with luck.

And it helped me realize something else: I had some value to provide him as well. It took me a few years to see it, but over time it emerged.

It started when I first asked him, "Why were you able to repetitively scale businesses to 100 million dollars or more?"

He would answer in a way relevant to the moment in time that I asked, and I would learn a great deal.

But then someone else would ask him a similar question a few weeks later, in a much different context, and he'd give another great answer—but it would be somewhat different from the one before, because the context of the question was different.

I saw this happen again and again. Kevin absolutely knew what he was doing, but he didn't know how to explain what he did based on a system or formula honed over decades of consistent results.

Yet the more time I spent with him, it was obvious that there *was* a formula to his entrepreneurial endeavors that he was using over and over and over again.

I became obsessed with figuring out exactly what it was. I made it a personal mission. How *was* he doing it?

It was so rare to see that kind of business success once, let alone twice—but more than 20 times? Nothing that happens that many times is accidental or coincidental. There was a pattern to how he was making this happen, and I was determined to figure it out.

What I discovered on this journey was nothing short of incredible. It was a master class in entrepreneurship and business that I did not think was even possible.

And this book is about sharing what Kevin has taught me with you.

I want you to experience what I experienced—not only how my mind-set about business changed, but how the way I interacted with my family changed as well.

My time with Kevin has dramatically and positively impacted the relationship I have with my children and my wife. Almost every relationship in my life is so much deeper and stronger today than it was before, when I was simply interacting with people by coming home to them as their dad and husband, compartmentalizing the entrepreneur in me.

What you're about to read is not just my interpretation of Kevin's words. I am going to take you on the journey with me, and you will hear Kevin's words out of his own mouth. My only role here is to help put it all together in a framework you can use in your life. I'll share how I was able to apply those lessons not only to myself, but to my businesses and my family.

I learned how to scale them both, my businesses as well as my family. I also learned how to scale a friendship—and, on this ride with me, so did Kevin.

CHAPTER ONE

BUT . . . WHY KEVIN?

Let's take a step back to my first phone calls with Kevin.

During one of those conversations, I sat at my kitchen table with my daughter Mary who was now 14. She fidgeted in her seat, until finally she smacked my arm.

"What?" I mouthed to her, covering the receiver.

"I want to talk to him!" she said in a loud whisper.

"No way," I said.

Mary pressed her palms together in a prayer position and stuck out her lower lip. "Please."

Kevin must have sensed my distraction. "Everything all right over there?"

I held up a finger to Mary. "Hey, yes, Kevin. I'm sorry. I'm sitting here with my daughter Mary and she's a bit of a fan and . . ."

"Is that right? Well, put her on the phone."

Mary must have heard him through the phone because our jaws simultaneously fell open. I hadn't dreamed of actually asking Kevin to speak to my teenage daughter, let alone let myself imagine that he might volunteer to talk to her. I went to hand Mary the phone and she shook her head.

"What do you mean, 'no'?" I whispered.

"What am I supposed to say?" she whispered back.

"You'd better figure it out," I said, and handed her the phone.

She slowly brought the phone to her ear. "Um. Hi. This is Mary."

Wanting to hear both sides of this conversation, I motioned for her to put him on speakerphone. She did and set the phone on the table.

"Hello, Mary. It's nice to meet you. I'm Kevin. So, what would you like to know?"

Mary looked at me with wide eyes. I waved my hand in a circle, urging her to speak.

"You were my favorite Shark on the show," she said. "Why did you leave?"

I had to admit, the question was an itch I'd wanted scratched myself.

"Great question, Mary. So, truth be told, not everyone who came on the show needed an investment—they just needed help. They needed advice and direction, and I wanted to give that to them even more than making an investment. Unfortunately, that wasn't what the show was about, and ultimately, I felt like I could do more for entrepreneurs outside of the program by providing them with the mentorship they needed to succeed. On the show there were, at best, dozens of businesses that I would be exposed to in a season. That wasn't enough—my desire was to be a mentor to millions!

"That said, Mary, I loved the show. It was a fantastic opportunity both for me and the entrepreneurs I got to work with. I wouldn't trade it for anything, but I had to do what felt right for me, which was creating a true win-win scenario for me and the entrepreneurs I encountered. And Mark Cuban is a great guy, and he came on and has done a really terrific job."

Mary had an ear-to-ear grin on her face—and so did I. The spark was lit for both of us. The fact that he would leave such a super successful show because of his desire to help up-and-coming entrepreneurs confirmed everything we had thought about Kevin. We knew then and there that Kevin was even more special than we had originally thought.

"Kevin, thank you for speaking with Mary," I said.

"And just so you know," Mary said, "I really do miss seeing you on *Shark Tank*!"

Kevin gave a hearty laugh and thanked her. I don't think Mary and I stopped smiling for the rest of the day.

Over the course of a few weeks, Kevin and I had more calls, and during that time, we decided to join forces to bring Zig Ziglar's legacy to the world together. It was becoming obvious that we liked each other. The fact that Zig was a mentor to both of us during our early adulthood gave us a common bond. The next step in forming a successful partnership was to get to know each other well and to ultimately trust each other. Talking on the phone all the time, though, was not going to get us to know, like, and trust each other.

So, I booked the family on a trip to Saint Petersburg, Florida.

Kevin and I had decided that the best way to extend Zig's legacy, since he had already passed away, was to share it as a *living* legacy through Kevin as the ultimate protégé of Zig. My idea was to interview Kevin so that I could understand at a deep level how Zig impacted him, and what he did with what he learned. I brought a small team and Mary with me to capture the content of the meeting.

Kevin decided the interview should be at his kitchen table. It was a long wooden one, and he sat at the end. We set up a recording device so that I could just focus on listening and asking him questions. I told him I thought this would take about an hour.

Boy, was I wrong about that.

TELL ME ABOUT "LITTLE KEVIN"

In all the years that Kevin had been interviewed, with those interviews likely numbering in the thousands, I had never seen or heard one that started with his childhood. I'd learned in my own entrepreneurial journey that there was no such thing as an overnight success, so even Kevin Harrington had to start *somewhere*.

To say he had me at "hello" would be something of an understatement.

"My mother was the daughter of Louis Kispert," Kevin began, "who was one of the original presidents of Fifth Third Bank. The bank started in Cincinnati with one location, and he was one of the top men in the organization. When he passed away, he left the family a lot of stock, which got divided up among his children—one of whom was my mother. My father, after he returned home from the war, became a restaurateur and an entrepreneur. So I came from this interesting background of finance and entrepreneurship.

"My mother wanted to live in this beautiful neighborhood that my dad couldn't afford. They ended up buying the cheapest house in the nicest neighborhood. I went to school with guys like Tommy Williams, who would later become the owner of the Cincinnati Reds, and Mark Everingham, whose father was the CEO and chairman of a large grocery store chain. At any rate, there was an old part of the street, and there was a new part of the street, and on the new part were the million-dollar houses. Guess which side we were on?" he asked, laughing.

"What do you think guys like Mark got on their sixteenth birthday? Old Mark's father gave him a Triumph—a TR6. What did I get when I was sixteen? I paid cash for an MG Midget because I wanted to keep up with the rest of my friends."

"Hold on," I said. "You paid *cash*? How did you get the money to do that?"

"I wasn't going to be given anything," Kevin said. "So I earned it."

CHIP OFF THE OLD BLOCK

"Let me get this straight," I said. "At sixteen, you earned enough money to pay cash for an MG Midget?"

"You're a pilot, right?" Kevin asked.

I nodded. At this point, he knew that I flew recreationally. "My father," he continued, "was a World War II hero. Flew in the Air Force. One hundred sixty-five missions. Now that's a lot, but it's even more when you consider that then, you were only required to fly twenty-five."

My jaw dropped open.

"I'll tell you more about that when we have more time," he said, "but suffice it to say, the man had no quit in him. When he finally returned home from the war and opened Harrington's Irish Pub, he was determined to teach me everything he knew. One of the first things he told me was, 'Kevin, you need to own your own business.' He was all about entrepreneurship, and all about teaching.

"I'll never forget, my dad told me once that the beer guy was going to be delivering kegs and he wanted me to count how many he brought in. The guy shows up and brings two kegs in and takes two empties back to the truck. He kept on this way for a bit—two in, two out. My dad comes walking through as he's going back to the truck and stops the guy.

"'Where are you going?' he asks him. 'Back to the truck with the empties,' the guy says. My dad takes one of the empties off another keg below it—and the bottom one is full. The guy was taking one full one and one empty back to the truck, trying to get over on the eleven-year-old watching him.

"'How did you know it was full?' I asked him. 'The keg was sweating,' he told me. 'You got to know what to look for. A sweaty, cold, full beer keg looks different than an empty one.'

"He wasn't just teaching me how not to get ripped off. He was teaching me how to look at things differently. Seeing the angles. And I worked twenty-hour shifts with him some nights. I was just immersed in all this.

"What's funny is that my mother was just the opposite. She said to me, 'You know you're not going down this entrepreneur path like your dad. He's in the bar business. He gets home at three A.M. You're going to be a banker, a lawyer, or a doctor.'

"I had two older sisters. One ended up marrying a doctor and the other a lawyer. I said to my mom, 'My grandfather's in the banking business. We got all the bases covered now.

"'I can be the entrepreneur.'"

THINK AND GROW RICH

At this point, our hour had turned into two.

I didn't care. I was fascinated—and so was Mary. We had to know more.

"Sunday was my dad's one day off from work. He worked from 11:00 A.M. until 2:30 A.M. the next morning, six days a week. On one of those Sundays, he opens up a box in front of me and pulls out a heat gun that's used for vinyl sealing. He tells me he's starting a vinyl sealing business.

"'Every restaurant has a problem,' he told me. 'They get tears and rips in the cushions of their seats. I'm going to start a repair business for them, and I want you to be a part of it.' And I was. We'd go out every Sunday, the man's only day off. Even when he was resting, he was hustling.

"He found out about lamination machines, and before I knew it, he had a bunch of them all over the city of Cincinnati, and I'd go collect the money from people using them. He bought the rights to Magic Fingers, the things that made the beds vibrate. We put them in all the Holiday Inns. This is what we did together, from the time I was eleven years old all the way up until college when I couldn't focus on that anymore.

"When we weren't out running those other businesses on a Sunday? He was sitting in his recliner with a stack of trade magazines and newspapers almost as tall as the chair itself. I asked him why he'd bother with all that when he was supposed to be relaxing. He told me he was looking for the hottest, latest, and greatest trends in restaurants. My dad was selling chicken wings long before there was WingHouse and Hooters. Every Friday night was wing night at Harrington's, and it was because he was spotting the trends.

"He was handing me all these journals, but the thing that really impacted me was when he handed me the book *Think and Grow Rich*. I remember getting so excited about what it taught me—that whatever you conceive and believe, you can achieve. Getting handed that book was like getting handed the keys to the MG. I told myself, *I'm going to do it. No one is going to do it for me, and I don't want them to, and there's not enough 'no's' in the world to keep me from doing it.*"

DRIVEWAY SEALING

Three hours later we were ordering Chick-fil-A to be delivered, and Mary and I scrapped all other plans for the day. We were just mesmerized. He kept going and we weren't about to stop him.

"At fifteen years old, I started my driveway sealing business," Kevin said.

"Fifteen?" Mary asked, wide-eyed.

"Fifteen," he said. "Like I said, I was motivated to have what my rich-kid friends had, but I was going to get it myself. One of the kids I went to school with, his family had been in the blacktop and driveway sealing business for thirty years, and they lived in one of those new, big mansions up the road. So my friend tells me that if I was thinking about a business, he could get the supplies.

"I first started riding my bike from house to house, knocking on doors. Twenty of them, to be exact. The first reaction was always, 'Who are you? Where's the owner of the company? Where's your dad?' They were thinking I was there to ask their kid to come out and play.

"Then my brother-in-law stepped up and said, 'Do mine for free, and I'll be your first testimonial.' I told him he had to cover the cost of the materials, which at the time was like eighteen bucks. He agreed, and we took before and after pics. I did a perfect job and put a sign up on his lawn. I got almost everyone signed up after that. I said that the first guy in the neighborhood to sign up only got charged twenty bucks, as long as I could take pictures like I did with my brother-in-law. The twenty people who said no at first? I got eighteen of them when I went back to them, then charging a hundred bucks a pop. I showed them the magical transformation that I'd provided their neighbors, and they were hooked.

"We started scaling quickly, which meant we needed drums of sealant—which meant we needed a truck. I'm fifteen, with no driver's license. I bought a pickup with the money I had made, along with some fifty-five-gallon barrels, which saved us a ton because we were now buying sealant in bulk. We rigged the drums to spray the stuff directly from them onto the driveway, and we were doing these things like an assembly line. I was doing a thousand dollars a week in business. It's how I earned the money to buy that first car."

BABEE TENDA

"This is incredible, Kevin," I said to him. "Is there more?"
Of course there was—and he didn't skip a beat.
"Babee Tenda was something I sold when I was sixteen years old. It sold for about three hundred dollars back in the seventies. They were used in hospitals. Babies couldn't fall out of it, they couldn't tip it, and they couldn't fall down and strangle themselves."
"Wait," Mary said. "What was Babee Tenda?"
"They were safety high chairs," Kevin said.
I couldn't help myself. "You sold *baby high chairs*?"
"Absolutely," he said. "Bruce, the owner of the company, had the idea to put little boxes in the malls that offered the possibility of a free trip to someone pregnant with their first baby. They had to put their info in the box, and then I'd get sent out to the house to deliver the prize.

"Everybody won, by the way. They got a day cruise out of Miami. The guy who sold the chairs got a thousand tickets for three dollars, and maybe five people out of the thousand actually took the trip. When I showed up at their door, the husband and wife, they're skeptical. I'd tell them I needed five minutes to tell them about all the things in the box, along with five minutes to tell them all about Babee Tenda.

"Once they let me in—and almost all of them did—I'd ask them, 'What's the most dangerous piece of equipment in the house when you have your baby?' I had these articles that talked about how dangerous the high chair was. The phone rings, and the mother goes for it? The baby's reaching for momma, flips the high chair. Someone's at the front door? Baby slips down in the seat and chokes.

"Then I told them that Babee Tenda was used right here in Children's Hospital in Cincinnati, Ohio, and if they had just a few more minutes, I could tell them all about it.

"In the beginning, I was closing maybe one in five prospects. It was a one-day close situation. I told Bruce that if they needed the night to 'think about it,' ninety-nine percent of the time, that sale wasn't happening. He told me he saw my potential and that he was going to go with me on a call. That's when he taught me about 'isolating the objection.'

"What it entailed was pulling the actual objection out of them. If they told me they wanted to think about it, I'd re-pitch the product, then ask them if the facts I presented were the things they wanted to think about. Once they admitted it was about the money, that's when I was able to move in. It was no longer about the quality. That's when I could hit them with the financing, which we were offering at nine dollars a month.

"I was closing seventy percent of them with that. But there was a problem."

Mary and I were rapt. We leaned forward, heads in our hands, and said simultaneously, "What was it?"

"Returns," Kevin said. "Of the seventy I closed, fifty percent of them were sending the chairs back, which they were allowed to do within three days of the sale. Almost every time, what happened was the couple would call their parents and tell them they bought a three-hundred-dollar high chair. Then the parents would talk them out of it. Bruce taught me the answer for this, too.

"'Appeal to their pride,' he told me. So I'd go back and ask the couple if when they got married, did the mother pick the location? Did she choose the cake? Nobody liked having their pride challenged.

"Bruce taught me so much about sales. I had zero cancellations from that point on. I still use many of the lessons he taught me today."

RUST PROOFING

I should point out that Mary was only 14 at the time of this interview. For the trip she had brought her phone, her computer, and a book in case she got bored.

She never looked at any of them. She was hanging on Kevin's every word—like me.

Not only that, but as the day went on, she kept moving closer and closer to the conversation.

Meanwhile Kevin had gotten so excited about sharing his early experiences that he was standing up so he could share with more passion. It was like his memories were fuel to a rocket that was about to take off. And he did.

"After I purchased the MG, I get a phone call," Kevin continued. "The guy on the line is congratulating me on my new car, telling me it's one of the biggest investments that I'd make in my life. He goes on to tell me that in two or three years, I'll see rust coming up on the fenders, but he offers a service to protect them. Done in one day, guaranteed for life. Could he drop off a brochure in my mailbox? I agreed.

"He shows up at my door. It turns out he's the sales manager of the rustproofing company Guardian that had just opened up—and they'd done it in a pretty slick way. They opened up in seven gas stations all around the city, rented a bay the station wasn't using, and paid them a percentage of every rust-proofing job. It was like the Uber of rust-proofing.

"He sees me and is shocked. He thought I was in my thirties based on our phone call. He asked me where the car was, and when I showed him, he was shocked all over again. 'How'd you get this car?' he asked. I told him I'd had a driveway-sealing business and now I was a salesman for baby high chairs.

"'You're wasting your time,' he said. 'You've got to come run with the big boys. I can give you a dozen leads a day.'

"I ended up selling as many as thirty rust-proofing packages a *week*. I became the number one salesman in the region, coming back with five or six sales a day. I would show up with my car, showing them the results of their work on my own vehicle. Back then, cars weren't rust-proofed coming out of the factory, so showing them the before and after photos was really effective. Just like with the driveway sealing."

HVAC

I was in awe of all he had to tell us. It would never have occurred to me that he had started down this path so early—that the history of his journey was so rich and started long before he became the Kevin Harrington we knew today.

He had one more story to share to close out the day—and it was incredible.

"I didn't always work for myself," he said. "At one point I worked for Trane heating and air conditioning. They licensed their name to a local heating and air company, one that had been around for thirty years and became the Trane affiliate in the market.

"When I showed up for the interview, the guy told me they only hired full-time people, and that he hadn't realized I was just a high school student. 'Why'd you call the ad?' he asked me. 'Because I want to make some money,' I told him.

"I told him I'd done my research on Trane and that I knew it was a great product. I couldn't be at every meeting, but what I could guarantee was that I'd be selling every night, and in a month, I'd sell more than their average guys across the board. Once I'd shown him what I'd done with Babee Tenda and the like, he finally agreed. I was a senior in high school, working for Trane.

"I had six leads the first week. By the sales meeting at the end of that week, I had three sales at three grand apiece, where the next guy only had one. By the end of the month, I was teaching the other guys how to close.

"After six months of this, I discovered that Trane was subcontracting to the affiliate. So I did some math. The equipment cost on a three-thousand-dollar job was about five hundred bucks. I was only getting ten percent commission, so three hundred dollars, while they kept the rest. I knew then and there that I could do this myself.

"That summer, my first year in college, I started Tri State Heating and Cooling. Turns out that business name belonged to a man who had long retired and had been in business for thirty years. I told him my story, and he said he'd sell me the name, but it was going to be very costly."

Mary leaned in. "How much was it?"

Kevin smiled. "One dollar. And we had to let him ride around with our crew when we did installations."

Mary breathed out a sigh of relief.

"So I went from a new business to thirty years in business. Took out a full-page ad in the yellow pages and rented out answering services. We serviced the whole city. I went down to the courthouse and bought all the new homeowner lists, called the owners up, and gave them free furnace cleanings. We went from zero to a million dollars in sales in the first year. By year two, we had twenty-five employees."

Mary and I looked at each other openmouthed. We couldn't believe what we were hearing—and Kevin ate it up. He went on to tell us about how he eventually went on to sell the business to one of his top salespeople when labor and tough inspectors got to be too much for a 19-year-old college student to manage.

THE PIVOT

When Kevin sold his HVAC business, he made a pivotal mind-set change—one that would influence the way he did business forever and would turn him into that Entrepreneur's Entrepreneur, a name I gave him, as that is truly who he is.

"I decided after my experience with the HVAC company," Kevin told us, "that I didn't want to be all about that sales hustle anymore. I needed to find a new way to do business. I had cash from the sale, and I was a young entrepreneur, so the world was my oyster. I started down the rabbit hole of exploring every business opportunity there was out there. *Entrepreneur* magazine, *Income Opportunities* magazine, *BizOp Classified*—you name it. During this time, I met a guy, Neil Balter, who owned the California Closets company in L.A.

"Neil had sold a couple of franchises, and he told me that I should become a franchiser as well. He told me that he had a bunch of guys calling him from Ohio and asked me to sell a couple of his franchises for him until I found my path, and he'd pay me a commission on them.

"What happened was I'd talk to some of these people, but they weren't carpenters and ended up not being interested in Neil's deal. So I asked Neil if I could find something else for them. Neil gave me his blessing, and so I'd tell the prospect about the thirty other deals I'd seen doing my own research."

This was the beginning of how Kevin became a franchise broker. This was the birth of Franchise America.

"I started partnering with some of the franchisers, venturing with them," Kevin explained. "With that, I had to go get my real estate license and named my company Harrington Enterprises. In the process of selling these franchises, at the closing table, I'd discover that these people didn't have someone to do their books, or handle their incorporation, or take care of their legal needs. I realized these people needed more than my help buying businesses—they needed my help all across the board.

"I renamed my business The Small Business Center and it was a one-stop center, the world's first shared office space—we were the first WeWork! I rented space to lawyers and accountants and advertising agents and gave them access to all these franchisers. It was terrific.

"Right around this time, I had also read Zig Ziglar's *See You at the Top*. It was this creation of The Small Business Center, along with the inspiration and motivation I found in Zig's words there, that marked a pivot point for me. It changed my whole mind-set about how I'd do business—and I never looked back."

All in all, we spent the better part of *six* hours just talking about Kevin's life, how it all started, and ultimately why he does what he does—how he became the Entrepreneur's Entrepreneur. He spent the first 30 years of his life learning how to become a world-class entrepreneur—then he spent the next 30 years being that entrepreneur.

Now he plans to spend the *next* 30 years teaching others, sharing his formulas, and opening up his life so that others can learn from him. Kevin will not want to be remembered for what he has done, but for how many he has helped to do the same.

It's why we've written this book.

Once we finished that day, there was no question in my mind that I needed Kevin Harrington as my mentor, and I knew that someday this story—the real story—needed to be told. He was about more than just the stories we had all heard, such as the invention of the infomercial or being a founder of EO (the Entrepreneurs' Organization). There were so many more experiences he'd had leading up to that to learn from—and so many more after. His story was grounded in sealing driveways, his father, and where he really learned to sell—baby high chairs.

It was that last story that really intrigued me—the beginning of the mind-set shift that marked the jumping-off point for the massive success Kevin would achieve in his illustrious career.

I had to know more.

CHAPTER TWO

GET THE RIGHT MIND-SET

So much of what I learned from Kevin came from the fact that the more we worked together, the more personal access I had to him when no one else was around. We traveled together often and spent a great deal of time in hotels.

One of our earliest trips together came after we had been business partners for just a few months. At that point, we really didn't know each other all that well. After traveling all day by air from Tampa to California, we then drove to our hotel. Kevin was going to be the featured speaker at Wealth Bowl the next day, yet when we arrived to check in, sometime after 11 P.M., we were told the hotel only had one room—and it was for me.

The hotel had made an error and thought Kevin was arriving the day before. When he didn't show up, they canceled his reservation and gave his room to someone else. Now the keynote speaker of an event they were hosting didn't have a room, and the organizer of the event had already gone to bed and couldn't be reached. So I turned to the front desk as the clock behind the clerk was nearing midnight, and I asked where the nearest hotel was and could they help me get a room, because clearly I needed to surrender my room to Kevin.

"It's late, we are both tired. We'll just share the room," Kevin told the clerk.

"Oh, but . . . you need to know it only has the one king bed," the clerk said.

We hardly knew each other. Kevin traveled nonstop. He had his routine, and I had mine, but there we were. We had to make the best of an uncomfortable situation—and we did. Before heading off to rest, we both used our lifelong training in negotiations one last time with the front desk, and although we could not manage to get that extra room, we did manage to wrangle a room with two double beds instead of one king. And by the next day we had both been upgraded to suites—Kevin the presidential suite. I don't think I'd ever seen a hotel room that large in my life. It was instances like these that allowed us to get to know each other better and better. It was in these moments that I started asking questions. I saw that when he wasn't on camera was when he was at his most vulnerable. I heard stories I'd never heard before about his early days learning to sell that premium baby high chair to new parents, and about his father, a World War II hero.

While I learned by hearing all of these stories privately, traveling with Kevin allowed me to see him in action, negotiating deals and business transactions, on conference calls, and speaking at events. I saw how Kevin Harrington became *Kevin Harrington*, the Entrepreneur's Entrepreneur and business icon.

That's where I also began to see that there were actions, behaviors, and ways of thinking that showed in everything he did. There was a real secret to his success, and though he wasn't able to put words to it, I could. I found, very quickly, that I could articulate what it was he was doing repetitively that was responsible for so much of his success.

A Fair Deal

Kevin has an appetite for deals, but they must be fair. In fact, he has far more interest in making sure a venture is a fair deal than whether or not it's a good one. He and I have been involved in more than one good deal that wasn't necessarily the fairest, and in all honesty, they never worked out.

"Good deals are usually not a win-win situation," Kevin said. "Someone wins and someone loses, and as soon as the business scales, the losing end bows out and it's no longer scalable.

"Every year, without fail, I sit down with my son and business partner, Brian, to evaluate the businesses I'm invested in or a part of to ask, Hey, is this thing working out for everyone involved? Is this happening the way we thought it would? Did we build this in a way where everyone is getting their fair share of the rewards for the work, time, and money invested? Believe me, I've seen deals structured—even by me—where that isn't the case, and suddenly you've got two or more unhappy parties in a deal. That's unsustainable. If it's not working out—that is, if it isn't structured to be fair—I'll give the whole deal back to the entrepreneur. I will return my equity in the venture and tear up the contract.

"As I said, a deal that isn't fair isn't scalable. If you're the one getting the good side of the deal, everything is great for you, especially as the deal starts to scale. But if you're on the other end of that, you're going to start feeling taken advantage of and you won't want to move forward. That's where the scaling stops.

"We're wired from birth to look for the best deal. We brag and high-five about it when we get one. We can't wait to tell other people about it. But we better be okay with that being the only deal we get from that person or that business, because we're probably not going to get it again.

"It might be human nature, but it can't be for an entrepreneur. You should only want fair deals, because good deals don't scale."

EXPONENTIAL THINKING

Those who know Kevin from television as the inventor of the infomercial or the man who brought Tony Little, Arnold Morris, and Jack LaLanne into our living rooms don't realize that there is a much deeper formula that he uses to discover synergistic opportunities.

He has mastered the concept of what I call exponential thinking.

An exponent is the multiplication of itself, sometimes many times over if the exponent is greater than two. If an opportunity comes before Kevin that has a linear growth potential, he's not interested. He doesn't want to simply add something to something else. The only thing that intrigues him is *multiplying* value. Even before I could articulate the elements of exponential thinking that Kevin utilized, I could see that he was always looking for a multiplication of resources and synergy—that that was what he was most drawn to. If he found a venture that had this quality, then there was an instant attraction to it for him. If I had gone to him with a business idea and said, "I can give you an eight percent return on equity year over year for the rest of your life," he would have fallen asleep before I finished the conversation.

As I watched him seek these opportunities time and again, I understood at a deeper level that thinking exponentially was a mind-set for him. While it might come naturally for him, I know that I did not wake up one day with the ability to think in that manner. It requires an aggressive curiosity—something we'll discuss more in-depth in the next chapter—but it also requires a willingness to look for those fair deals we discussed earlier, where everyone wins.

"What You Vividly Imagine . . ."

Kevin told me that he begins and ends his day with one quote from personal development pioneer Paul J. Meyer:

"What you vividly imagine, ardently desire, sincerely believe, and enthusiastically act upon, must inevitably come to pass."

If I had to succinctly frame Kevin's life, it would be summed up in those 17 words. That quote encapsulates the mind-set that has led to his enormous success—to becoming the Entrepreneur's Entrepreneur. So let's examine that quote a little bit closer.

You must *ardently desire* that which you vividly imagine. You can't just go into any venture haphazardly, strolling into it ho-hum. You have to be passionate about wanting to solve that problem. Kevin typically chooses ideas that are solutions for problems that need to be solved. When many people are looking to have something solved for them, it's quite easy to ramp up your desire to help them solve it.

In order to do that, though, you must *sincerely believe* in it.

"So often," Kevin said, "someone will seek me out, asking me to endorse their product. I tell them, 'Send me some samples, because I have to use it. If you're telling me this new supplement will allow you to work ten hours longer per week with greater productivity, then send it to me so I can try it, because if I don't sincerely believe it, then I'm not going to embrace it, and I'll have no desire to push it.'"

Once you have the ardent desire, and once you sincerely believe in what you've allowed yourself to imagine, you must enthusiastically act upon your goal as though it's going to be achieved, understanding that likely you will fail—and fail multiple times before it comes to pass.

Taking enthusiastic action is the missing piece that determines and separates the wildly successful from the not so successful. So many entrepreneurs want to imagine, desire, and believe, with the thought that those three elements alone will bring their success about. It simply doesn't work that way. When you enthusiastically act upon those ideas, it is then—and only then—that success can occur, because action allows for failure. Once you fail, then you know if you've got a good idea or a bad idea, or you learn and you emerge stronger, like a phoenix from the ashes, a concept we will take a deep dive on later in the book.

FEAR

There is only one path to making good decisions—first making bad ones. However, so many of us are terrified of making bad decisions, and as a result, we don't act.

The number one thing holding any entrepreneur back is fear. Fear of failure, fear of success, and fear in general. Kevin taught me about this extensively. He believes in the power of mentors and coaches to navigate those fears. We simply don't have the resolve to do it ourselves.

"My son Brian worked with me in some of my ventures," Kevin told me. "He would get so discouraged because we would get involved in these products and would see failure after failure after failure. But then one out of those ten would hit and go to a hundred million. I'd ask him, 'Would you rather have ten products we select all do a million dollars, or would you like to see one of those ten do a hundred million?' I mean, that's pretty simple math, right? The question becomes, How much can we learn from the other nine so that we find that one that makes one hundred million?

"Because Brian was young, he still had that fear of failing, whereas I was not afraid to try new things because I knew the only path to the one-hundred-million-dollar idea was through numerous failures. Most people say to themselves, *Oh, I've got this great idea. Let's go succeed!* That's the wrong mind-set.

"Instead, tell yourself, *This is a great idea. Let's go fail at it. Let's fail as fast as we can and see if here is something we can learn, even if that something is that there isn't anything to learn. That there's nothing to be gained.* If you can fail fast and learn, then you have a chance to pivot and be successful. But speed is key. If it takes you a long time to fail, you might use up all of your cash thinking you've got a great idea, only to fail and have nothing left to rise from."

THE PROCRASTINATING PERFECTIONIST

"Failing doesn't mean spending or losing a lot of money," Kevin continued. "That idea is why so many people become what I call procrastinating perfectionists.

They're so attached to the notion of making their idea perfect, when the truth is there is no such thing as a perfect idea. If your concept is more than 80 percent done, you've taken it further than you should. Deploy your idea and let the marketplace take care of the last 20 percent. You've got to enthusiastically act."

It reminded me of a story Zig Ziglar once told that I knew had resonated with Kevin as it did with me—the story of Roger Bannister.

From the time humans started tracking how fast someone was able to run a mile, no one had been able to do it under four minutes. In fact, physicians once said that it was physically impossible because the heart would literally explode. Then one day, after almost 70 years of experts and naysayers purporting this impossibility, Roger Bannister ran a mile in under four minutes.

Now, while this feat was amazing in and of itself, what happened next was even more incredible.

In that same year, *after* Roger Bannister set this incredible record, seven more people did the exact same thing.

For 70 years, no one could do it—then Roger Bannister does it and seven more people follow suit. How was this possible? The only reason that makes sense is because now people knew it could be done. What was once believed impossible was now no longer so. In the years following, hundreds of thousands of people broke the four-minute-mile barrier.

Zig's point in telling this story is that we limit ourselves until we know and believe something is possible. It is the fatal flaw of the procrastinating perfectionist. They work and work on their idea until they believe it's 100 percent ready to bring to market, because they feel it's the only way it will be guaranteed to work. They want so badly to start their venture, but because everyone tells them it can't be done—because they've seen so many try and fail before them—they believe the only way it can be accomplished is if it's perfect.

It's why when Kevin meets these budding entrepreneurs, he asks them: How much do you desire solving this problem? How much do you believe that the world needs the solution to this problem? How vividly can you imagine what the world would be like if this problem is solved? If they can answer these questions, then all that's left is for Kevin to share his experiences documented in this book to show them that it *can* be done.

Stop the daydreaming. Stop creating prototypes to cover all the possibilities. Stop telling people about your idea. You can have a billion-dollar idea in your head, but if you don't put it into the world, it's not worth two nickels.

Act on it. Run toward success.

Not Just a Business Mind-Set

The more time I spent with Kevin, the more I found I was gut-checking myself. In my entrepreneurial ventures, I'd ask myself: *Is this only a good idea because I think I can make money? Or is this an idea that I ardently desire and sincerely believe in?* This isn't to say that there's anything wrong with an idea with which you can earn money—but if that's your sole motivation, then the notion is handicapped from the beginning.

I know because I've seen it in my own life.

Back before I had Kevin as a mentor, whenever I chased the dollar, it rarely materialized because I didn't have the mind-set Kevin would later instill in me. I had to believe that there was a problem the world needed solved and that I was the person to solve it, and I had to have the passion to do so. When I didn't, I stalled out. Not only did I not make money, I lost it.

I learned that this mind-set applied to my family life as well. You can't do what I call the "Facebook family" thing. It's where you're scanning Facebook, seeing all of these "perfect" families, and trying to implement all the things they're doing with your own family. The same principles that Kevin taught me about business are relevant here. If you don't ardently desire and sincerely believe in those things those other people are doing, you won't enthusiastically act upon them. They will be hollow attempts at interacting and bonding with your loved ones, and as a result, they will ultimately fail.

How many families sit around the kitchen table and talk about their future and then do nothing to get there? So many of them never have an on-purpose, intentional, scheduled family meeting—*ever*. The only time they meet is in the upstairs hallway talking about their schedules for the next day, or at dinner with their iPhones out, barely paying attention to each other about who's doing what and when.

In business, we meet every week, or we don't function. We take that time to talk about who we are, what we stand for, and why we're in business to begin with; about how we satisfy our customers and our community; about our purpose and how we live it.

Why aren't we doing this with our families? It's the rarest ones who sit down together and say, "We're not an accident. We were put here for a reason. Let's start sincerely and ardently believing that and do something about it as a family. That means we're going to have to act intentionally—to run our family like it's a business. Like it matters."

That's the only way it works.

When I sat in my car in my driveway and had the epiphany I told you about in the beginning of this book, I didn't yet have an entrepreneurial mentor in Kevin. If all I did was take what I learned in business back to my family, I knew I was going to be selling them short, because there was still so much for me to learn about being an entrepreneur that I needed to apply to my business before I ever tried to apply it to my family.

Working with Kevin has drastically changed the way I'm able to integrate my time at work and with my children. In the earliest stages of my travels with Kevin, I had the opportunity to bring another one of my daughters, Cassandra, with me to see a brainstorming session between me and Kevin. Cassandra was 14 years old and was about to begin her freshman year in high school. I had my laptop open, and in the middle of a very intense conversation with him, I see an e-mail flash on the screen. It's from Cassandra.

I don't typically look at my e-mails in moments like those. I like to give my full attention to the person with whom I'm speaking—but my daughter had sent me this message while she was sitting 10 feet from me at Kevin's kitchen table. I had to open it. It read:

Dear Mr. Timm—

It has come to my attention that you are in great need of a personal assistant. I happen to know someone that I think could be qualified for this position. If you'd like to explore this in greater detail, you can reach me at this address or at my cell phone number.

Sincerely,
Cassandra Timm

I immediately forwarded the e-mail to our human resources department—no, really, our *actual* human resources department—and told them I'd like to have this young lady interviewed to be my personal assistant. After we returned home from our trip to visit Kevin, she came in, dressed in sharp business attire, and interviewed with my VP of operations. She then ultimately interviewed with me.

"The challenge, Cassandra," I said, "is that I love your enthusiasm, and you've impressed a lot of people along the way. But to be my personal assistant, you would not be able to go to public school. I travel extensively, and this wouldn't be possible."

To my surprise she said, "I've already thought about that and had a conversation with Mom. I'm prepared to drop out of public school and take classes at an online academy for a year so that I can travel as your personal assistant."

I hired her on the spot.

Since then, she's traveled with me on 30 different trips and learned how to take notes. It got to the point where I could go into meetings and never have to open my laptop. I would get a bullet-pointed document detailing a schedule of what both I and everyone else in that meeting had committed to. She had the opportunity to meet extraordinarily amazing human beings from all over the planet— famous people Kevin knew, including multimillionaires and billionaires.

Best of all, we got to develop a relationship that wouldn't have been possible in any other way—and it wouldn't have been possible without Kevin Harrington.

By doing business with me and by embracing my children on these trips, he expanded my mind as to what was possible in my family. Originally, what I sought to learn from him as an entrepreneur was how to scale, because I had never successfully scaled a business beyond $10 million, where Kevin had taken multiple ventures to $100 million.

However, I also hadn't figured out how to scale my family.

Taking the kids on a trip here and there was me being an entrepreneur. What I did that year with Cassandra—having her leave public school, enroll in an online academy, and travel as my personal assistant—that's scale.

Real scale is sustainable. It's not someone coming along and giving you an order for $100,000 one month, and then next month you only make $1,000. That's a one-time lucky order. It is *not* scale. True scale is when you experience exponential growth that is sustainable. That year that Cassandra traveled with me was loaded with exponential growth. She had exposure to amazing people, opportunities, and careers, as well as different parts of the country and the world. She couldn't un-see what she saw—couldn't unlearn what she learned. She had forever altered her trajectory.

We normally measure a business's scale in terms of increased sales or bottom-line dollars. Cassandra scaled by increasing her wisdom, experience, and desire. It's the kind of thing parents can only hope for their children and their family.

Kevin helped me to tap into the vivid imagining of what my family could be if I ran it like a business. I had the desire and the sincerity to do so, but Kevin gave me the permission to enthusiastically act upon all of it at a level I had held myself back from.

"You Can Have Everything . . ."

Remember that Zig Ziglar line Mary quoted to me? It was actually quite famous:

> "You can have everything in life you want if you'll just help enough other people get what they want."

We spend so much time trying to come up with the next best idea, when in reality, if we help someone get what they want—if we help them make their vision a reality—they might then spend the rest of their lives selling us to others.

Kevin lives this mind-set and has done it for countless people. He doesn't have to go looking for the next greatest idea. He has so many people out there now looking for him, looking for ideas for him simply because he was fair and did good business with them. Later in this book, I'll tell you how Kevin shared with me that the person who turned out to be one of his biggest success stories was looking for deals and ideas to send to Kevin while he was, quite literally, on his deathbed.

It speaks loudly to the relationships Kevin builds with his mind-set and approach to doing business. He's passed that mind-set on to me, and it's changed me and the relationships I hold dear in my life—forever.

Have you ever seen a turtle on a fence post? If you have, there is one thing you can determine with absolute certainty—that turtle didn't get up there by himself. Someone had to put him there. Now, if you're thinking a bit too hard about this image, you might imagine it's a negative—like, the turtle is now stranded on that fence post, helpless. But I'm not talking about that, I'm looking at it in a positive light: the turtle is in a higher place he never could have got to on his own.

Kevin has often been the man putting that turtle on the post—you just didn't know it.

I've taken that concept back to the business of my family.

During our family meetings, if you did something really well, instead of standing up in front of us and receiving a standing ovation, we want to know how the turtle got on the post. Who put you there? Who influenced you? Was it Grandpa Larry? A friend from school? A teacher or a coach? Who is responsible for getting you there, can you articulate how they did it, and then can you tell them thank you?

On the flip side, if our children made a bad decision—they got a speeding ticket, for example, or they wrecked the car—well, that's another kind of fence post. It's not a fun one to be on, but they still need to be able to communicate how they got there. Who told you to go fast on that road just because it would be fun? Who influenced you to have that drink when you knew better?

At last count, there are 40 fake turtles scattered around our home in various places. The turtle isn't just about being congratulatory. When you make bad decisions, chances are somebody had a great role in helping you get on that post as well, and it's equally important to identify those who have a harmful influence as it is to determine those who are helpful.

In many ways, this relates to Kevin's exponential thinking. We have to have the mind-set where we're asking ourselves, *How do I exponentially impact other people by solving their problem, so that they can in turn exponentially impact me?*

It is my feeling that Kevin Harrington will never have to have another original idea for the rest of his life. He's put so many turtles on fence posts that they're shouting about him and for him at the tops of their lungs, "If you have a great idea, talk to Kevin Harrington!" When you sincerely help 100 people get what they want, and those 100 people tell 10 people about it that also have that problem, you've just 10x'ed your business. It's why Kevin has access to some of the most extraordinary opportunities, because he has helped so many entrepreneurs that they can't help but promote him and enthusiastically share stories about their experiences with him.

I'm constantly blown away, even years later, at the access to deal flow—people bringing exceptional opportunities to Kevin—that he has, and it's not an accident. He's taken a lifetime to create this channel, and it's come from having done right by the right amount of people. I've witnessed it firsthand. I've seen him do it, and I've seen the results. I've seen how it flows back to my life both as an entrepreneur and a family man.

Kevin doesn't do alone, either. He has numerous mentors, and knowing that gave me permission to bring more mentors into my life whom I can turn to when I need help, guidance, or advice. It's one of the biggest gifts Kevin has given me—to allow myself to bring mentors in my life, and to say to them with enthusiasm and without the hesitation of embarrassment, "I need your help. You know things I don't know, and I can learn from you." In doing so, I've become a mentor to others. It's a full-circle process.

It can be lonely as an entrepreneur. We get misinformed somehow that to be one, we have to do this alone—but if you surround yourself with mentors and advocates, you greatly increase your odds of seeing fantastic success.

That's admittedly a huge mind-set change, but one that is absolutely crucial for you to make.

The one thing that we both hope comes screaming loudly throughout this book is that not only is mentorship necessary, it's also more readily available than you realize, and it's one of the biggest parts of Kevin's formula for success. Whenever Kevin throws himself into a new venture or category with which he's not familiar? The first thing he does is find a mentor.

If he can do it, so can you.

This book is my shout from the top of the fence post.

CHAPTER THREE

AGGRESSIVE CURIOSITY

Kevin and I decided to accelerate our relationship together. I was in a flexible stage in life as an entrepreneur and had even found a little bit of margin with my family. We're used to using *margin* as a business term, but in the business of family, margin equals time. The reality is that children spell *love* t-i-m-e. We can look at our lives as though we have "no time" or as though we have 24 hours in a day. Many entrepreneurs find themselves in this spot—where their business is taking over their lives and they simply don't have any margin.

Since Kevin and I had a great deal of traveling and work to do together, to further this margin we'd identified, my wife and children and I decided that for one month, we'd live where Kevin did, in Saint Petersburg, Florida. Being that we lived permanently in Indiana, it didn't take much arm-twisting to get them to agree to head south in

January. It might have been one of the easiest conversations I'd ever had with my family.

Making the decision to be where Kevin was for a full month—to be completely available to him, to be in his home, to travel with him—took our mentor–mentee relationship to an entirely different level. We interacted through the holidays and spent time with his family. It brought us closer as friends and solidified our working relationship.

"Do You Know Anything about Holograms?"

During my time there, inspiration struck.

As I've mentioned, the great Zig Ziglar was my mentor, and he was Kevin's as well. As Kevin and I embarked on this journey about how we could resurrect and maintain Zig's legacy, he had an idea.

What if we could take footage of Zig Ziglar and turn it into a hologram?

The thought was that if we could do that, we could conceivably show up to a speaking event, talk about the impact Zig had on our lives, and then have him appear on stage with us in holographic form.

The idea sounded great in theory. Once Kevin had an idea, though, his aggressive curiosity drove him to find out as much as he possibly could to see if it was possible to bring that idea to life. At every event he attended, he'd ask people if they knew anything about holograms. It didn't matter who they were or what they did; he was going to ask until he found someone who knew something, because he knew eventually someone would—and he was right.

He was first referred to a company in California that did some work for Hollywood. They wanted $100,000 to take the Ziglar footage and convert it to a hologram that Kevin could use onstage. Not only that, but they also required another $25,000 every time he wanted to use it on stage.

For anyone else, that would have been game over—no dice. Most people would tell themselves that if this company was going to charge that much, it was unlikely that any other company would be any more affordable, and they would give up the ghost of pursuing the idea any further. I abandoned the notion. Kevin's son, who Kevin had involved in the project, did as well.

Kevin didn't. The setback only kicked his aggressive curiosity into overdrive. He asked everyone, everywhere we went, to the extent that the whole thing became something of a running joke. We'd always say that each time, he was getting one step closer to making it a reality.

Then it wasn't a joke anymore.

Kevin met someone at yet another event, and that someone had a friend who knew a guy who was the relative of a man who owned a hologram company in Toronto. After speaking with them on the phone, they invited us to come up to their facility not only to see their technology, but to be turned into holograms ourselves. We also sent them the Ziglar footage so they could have a demonstration ready for us when we arrived—all at a fraction of the cost of the California studio.

As impressive as all of this was, it was on our plane to Toronto where I truly witnessed Kevin's aggressive curiosity in action.

THE TRASH BAG

The flight was scheduled for the end of the day. As I was living down in Florida with my family, Kevin and I didn't travel to the airport together. When we arrived, I noticed that Kevin had his usual blue Louis Vuitton bag with him, one that I'd recognize anywhere.

But then I noticed a second bag—one I'd never seen before.

It was bulging like it was jam-packed with—something. My curiosity was piqued. *What is in that bag?* I reasoned to myself that it was his overnighter—until I saw that he had his carry-on suitcase as well. It had me scratching my head in wonder at what exactly was going on.

Our seats were in first class, right at the bulkhead. After takeoff, Kevin got up out of his seat and brought the mystery bag down from the overhead compartment. Inside were a countless number of newspapers, magazines, and trade journals. As I sat next to him going through my e-mails, Kevin was tearing through these publications— literally. Each time he found something that interested him, he'd rip out a page of the magazine and put it in a folder. When he finished the magazine, he'd toss it on the floor.

The next thing I knew, there was a good-size pile in front of him. He was going through these things like a machine, totally in the zone. Admittedly, I was a bit taken aback. At one point I asked myself, *What is going on?* Was this man showing me some strange side of him I hadn't seen yet? Right around that time, the flight attendant came by. As if she were in on the whole thing, she brought a trash bag, just for him. In it she stuffed all the newspapers and journals piled in front of him until it was almost filled to bursting, just so he could keep going.

The flight from Tampa to Toronto was approximately three hours. In that time frame, Kevin got through the *entire bag.* He whittled all of it down to a folder of content. I didn't want to interrupt his process—whatever it was—because while he was doing his thing, I was doing mine with my own work. Once we were both done, I closed my laptop and turned to him.

"All right," I said. "I've got to know. That was quite an experience I just witnessed. What *were* you doing?"

"I subscribe to multiple newspapers," he said. "Multiple trade journals and magazines. Oftentimes, I get so busy when I'm home that I don't have time to read them, so I save them up and get through them while I travel."

"But you went through that whole bag in three hours. That was a week's worth of reading. Are you a speed reader?"

"Not at all," he said. "I just know what I'm looking for."

He said it as if that should be end of it—as if I should know what it was he was looking to find.

"All right," I said, laughing, "I'll take the bait. What are you looking for?"

"I just want to see where the eyeballs are going," he said.

I told him I didn't know what he meant by that. The truth was that I did to some extent, but I knew this would be an incredible teaching moment for me, and I wanted to wring all I could from it. He didn't disappoint.

"Look, if you look at where I started out," he said, "the reason I'm still relevant and that I've been able to stay in this business is because I've developed an ability to follow the eyeballs. What are the trends? What are people looking at? Where are people spending their time? I made billions of dollars in sales in cable television with the infomercial, right? Google 'cable television subscribers' today, though, and you'll see that people are shedding their cable bill like nobody's business. Sometimes cable services drop as many as a million subscribers in a single month. Cable TV is going down, down, down—but we have more people consuming more media than we've ever consumed in the history of . . . of consumption! So where are the eyeballs? Where are they going?

"I ask myself, *What are people interested in?* This is the product side. I'll sit down and Google the top-selling items on Amazon. That information is readily available. I want to see what people are buying and where. Then I hit my magazines, newspapers, and journals. If I see an ad showing up in more than one trade journal, then I know it's something that's working—that it's got legs in that niche market. Nobody runs repetitive ads if they aren't generating results. Instead of looking at all the content, I look at who's advertising and what they are selling. Then I ask, If someone is having success in print media, is it something that can live on QVC? Can it be taken to digital? Sometimes I look for new product ideas that aren't even in categories I'm focusing on."

In my mind, I slapped my forehead, as if to say, "Of course." It was so simple, but it was genius in its simplicity. I asked Kevin how he came to this style of aggressive curiosity. Was it natural? Was it something he developed over time? The more I got to know him, particularly his life story, it became clear to me that this curiosity grew from the journey he had taken up to this point.

However, it was never clearer to me than when he explained how he came to what would be the most pivotal point of his entrepreneurial career.

Six Hours of Dead Air

Kevin thought back to the beginning of his "second 30 years of life," when he began talking to people about being a business broker—someone who sold franchises or helped people buy businesses. It was the birth of Franchise America.

"The idea really piqued my curiosity," he said. "It was like: whoa, wait a minute—there are people out there who actually help people buy businesses like the ones I'm seeing in these trade journals?

"I had some money from the heating and air-conditioning company I'd sold. Instead of buying another business, I started a business brokerage, a kind of 'first of its kind.' Keep in mind, I was just in my twenties, but this brokerage put me on the front cover of *Entrepreneur* magazine. It was kind of my arrival in the business world.

"It was all about the idea of saying, What if I can help you? There were all of these people out there like me who wanted to be an entrepreneur but didn't know how. They didn't know how to start a business. They didn't know where to turn for help.

"So, I went to franchisors like Subway, and I would sell their franchise *for* them, and I would get a commission from them for doing so. As I did this more and more, it led to a partnership with *Entrepreneur* magazine, and the business eventually became the Entrepreneur Franchising Center. We ended up putting these franchise locations all over the country. People would come in and look through brochures from fifty to a hundred different business opportunities, and I would help them pick the right one for them."

This all arose from Kevin's curiosity. He started out as most do, by buying businesses of his own—yet there was a drive within him to do and learn more. It was far more educational for him to help others get into businesses than it was for him to buy a franchise of his own. He could have bought five franchises for himself and done just fine, but he was fascinated with the amount of people like him who wanted to be entrepreneurs.

Not only did it drive his curiosity, it sparked his altruistic nature. He decided that the thing he wanted to do was to help others get their dream businesses by being the broker for these franchises. Not only did he make both sides of the equation happy, he satisfied his curiosity—at least temporarily—by learning more about other entrepreneurs in the process.

Those who think they know Kevin's story think that products like the Ginsu knives and the Gazelle and all those early successes were the birth of the infomercial.

They weren't.

The original start for Kevin was his getting a franchise to record a 10-minute advertisement about their franchise. He'd get three of them to come together, and he'd hire a team to produce a 30-minute segment about the three different businesses. Then Kevin bought television time— and it was his aggressive curiosity that led him to find that time in the most ingenious of ways.

"One night, late, I was surfing through the TV channels, and I landed on the Discovery Channel," Kevin said. "I'm seeing nothing but multicolored bars. Now, you know me, Mark. I paid for television shows, I want television shows, even if I'm not going to watch them. So I picked up the phone and called the cable company. I said, 'Hey, I'm getting ripped off here. I'm paying you for shows and I've got bars across my screen. What's going on?' They say, 'Oh, sorry, sir, but the Discovery Channel is new. They only have so many hours of programming, so whenever they don't have anything to show, they just put up those bars for six hours.'

"Now, at this time, I've already got a network of all of these entrepreneurs who want to start businesses, along with a network of franchisers who want to find them— and they've all got a subscription to cable, just like me.

I asked myself, *What if I used those bars on the screen and turned them into infomercials of franchise opportunities for entrepreneurs?*

"I went down to the cable operator, and they told me they had a huge charter inside the company to empower local entrepreneurs. They had a huge production studio. I asked them, 'What if I do a thirty-minute show called *Own Your Own Business*, and I feature businesses for sale?' They loved the idea and said they'd work up a budget. I thought it would be thousands of dollars—it was eight hundred dollars. I said, 'Where do I sign?' I hired the co-anchor from NBC News to cohost with me for an additional two hundred fifty dollars, and we put out a press release in the *Cincinnati Enquirer*.

"We got four hundred fifty leads from thirty airings of the show. We sold four businesses and made an average of six grand from an investment of one thousand fifty dollars."

"That's incredible," I said.

"It gets better," Kevin told me. "From there, we took it national with the *Franchise America* show. I told those national companies to pay me ten grand and I'd have three of them on per show at ten minutes each. That got me thirty grand for production. We were outbound telemarketing franchise companies and closing them like crazy because they're seeing the show on national television.

"But how I was going to sell for thirty minutes? Well, around the same time as this was happening, Zig Ziglar's book *Secrets of Closing the Sale* had been released. In it were more than 100 different closing techniques. I used that as my formula to draft the script for our thirty-minute segments, and I would use between twelve and twenty closes in a single pitch.

"What people don't realize is that we typically don't buy until after the fifth close, but most salespeople only use one to two. A thirty-second advertisement is only one to two closes—a call to action. Using up to twenty in those thirty-minute segments was how I became so successful, using a variety of the techniques Zig had taught me through his book.

"And as such, the infomercial was born."

WHAT'S THE PROBLEM?

Being curious, I'd learn, wasn't enough. When it came to Kevin's quest for new businesses and products to get behind, it was crucial that he knew what problem they solved. That concept became a constant for him. For something to truly grab and hold his attention, it had to solve a problem—if nothing else, for scalability. A product couldn't just be a "nice-to-have." If he was able to find people who had a particular issue and he could connect them to a product that had a way to solve it, there was a really good chance he'd invest his time, money, and energy in it. It had to provide that "magical transformation."

"Take OxiClean," Kevin said. "Here is my wife with this stain that's going to ruin her favorite outfit forever. Maybe it had some sentimental value, or it was rare and expensive—whatever—$9.95 worth of OxiClean, and she can keep something that held meaning for her.

"Proactiv, the acne solution. There's this picture of a poor teenager with acne from their head to their toes. They're probably bullied, having trouble finding a boyfriend or girlfriend—heck, severe acne can even be painful. And here's this formula that can give them that magical transformation that literally changes their life. The value of something like that far exceeds the actual price.

"I look for those kinds of attributes in a product. I travel a lot, and my bag is a mess of charging cords. It can be a real pain, but the world is such today that we can't live without our technology. We have to stay charged to keep ourselves in the game. People have tried to solve for it with these portable power packs and what have you, but those didn't capture my attention. You still have to have a cord. To me, those don't solve the real problem.

"What if you could walk into a building, your house, or your car and look down at your phone to see that it's charging? No cord. Just charging. What kind of problem would that solve for you? Imagine going into your favorite restaurant with your battery low and being fully charged by the time you left.

"There's a company working on this right now. You better believe that one got my attention, and now I own a piece of it!"

Sharpen Your Axe

Immersing myself in Kevin's world had an intense effect on my own curiosity. To this day, I'm constantly trying to see around the corner the way he does.

There used to be a time when I'd go to an event, and the questions I'd ask myself were, *What time do I have to speak? What time am I done? What time do I have to leave to get to the airport on time?*

Then I started thinking about Kevin.

Kevin would ask himself, *Who's going to be at this event whom I can talk to who might be a new contact or a new resource—a link to a new product or idea?* No matter where he went, he was always willing to do these types of meetings, even when some of them would come up empty.

"But you've only got to be right one out of ten times," he said.

That situation with the trash bag full of trade journals also had a profound influence on the way I spend my time. If Kevin Harrington has the time to be curious and read through stacks and stacks of magazines and papers, then so do I—and so do you.

If you start doing your research, you'll realize that all the greats do this. Warren Buffett spends three to four hours a day feeding his curiosity about companies and financial markets. He's an avid reader. Same with Bill Gates. Most entrepreneurs share the trait of curiosity, but it tends to be narrow in focus—only in their area of expertise. The super successful have an insatiable appetite for information about even seemingly unrelated topics, because they know if they don't, they might miss out on the next big opportunity, and they are intentional about the time they take to find those opportunities.

I was quite guilty of the "I don't have time" excuse. The truth is that you can't keep chopping away at the tree knowing that your axe is so dull that it's not cutting anything. You have to take the time to sharpen your axe. Sharpen it to such an edge so that when you swing, it takes half the effort to bring that tree down.

Kevin doesn't have as intimate a working relationship with the teams that are behind his business ventures as I do. So I've found myself also being more curious around my staff and my team, spending more time asking them questions and mining them for their thoughts and views to discover what they're learning, and empowering them to bring their best to the table and share more. I've seen very real results from this.

I thought my job as a leader was to solve my teams' problems. It was a mind-set I was entrenched in. If someone had a problem, I wanted him to bring it to me to fix it.

Being curious and asking questions, I learned that my *real* job was to help *them* learn how to solve their own problems.

So many leaders function in the "I'll fix it for them" mind-set, but it's so important to remember—give a man a fish, and he'll eat today; teach him to fish, and he'll eat for the rest of his life. I wasn't curious enough to figure out if my teams had the capacity to solve their problems. I knew I was good at it, but by asking questions, I learned that my teams were better at it than I was. If they had to fix things my way, then they had to learn my way. When they solved them on their own, they did it in ways intuitive to them.

Oftentimes our methods differed, but theirs were better because they were sustainable and scalable, because they made sense to them instead of just making sense to me. Looking back, I saw that my solutions were inefficient, but they were doing what I told them simply because I was the boss—even when it wasn't in the best interest of our financial bottom line.

Making this realization has given me back margin in my life, because if you're the only person solving problems, then your business cannot run without you. I was spending 80 or 90 percent of my time *in* the business, and the rest of the time working *on* the business. Now it's the inverse. I am there when they hit a roadblock, and it's still not in a capacity to solve things for them. I provide them with the right information or talk to the right person, which allows them to take the necessary next steps.

There was a time when we struggled with our financial reporting because we were doing it the way I knew how to do it. What I should have been doing was empowering my team to do it the way they wanted to, but I wasn't curious enough about their thoughts and opinions. When I finally got out of their way and asked them, How they would do it? I got the financial reports on time and more accurate than they ever were before.

My paradigm has been flipped. Whereas I once felt I didn't have the time to be curious, I now realize I can't afford *not* to be curious. How could I begin to consider myself an entrepreneur if I wasn't willing to invest in the research and the reading—to see what my competitors were doing and what was happening in the marketplace? What did it say about me that I was another amateur lumberjack, whacking away at the tree with my dulled axe? Was I even chopping down the right tree?

Two Ears and One Mouth

Perhaps more importantly, I've seen the effect of my curiosity on my family. Too often we go through the motions of life without stopping to ask, Why are we doing this? Why are we doing what we're doing, and what *should* we be doing? How can we be a better family, better parents and children, and have a stronger marriage?

I think through my curiosity with my family, and it's helped me to learn to listen. There's a saying I love: God gave us two ears and one mouth for a reason. We need to listen twice as much as we speak. You can't be curious and talk. You have to receive input. In engaging with my family about how I can be more of the dad that they want me to be, it became quite obvious to me that I had the reputation of being a workaholic and that they didn't have my undivided attention.

I'm still a work in progress in this regard, but in listening to them, I've worked quite hard on what I do with my "free time." It is still quite difficult for me to have focused free time, meaning I don't work in those periods—I don't answer my phone, I don't respond to e-mails. It's still such a process that I can't even be near my phone during that time because I'm just too tempted to look.

Do you want to be held accountable? Tell your kids that you want to be all in, focused on them when you put them to bed at night, and if you look at your phone, give them permission to take it away from you or even penalize you in some way. They will feel like the most empowered creatures on planet Earth. The first time I screwed up, they were all over me. It was embarrassing, in the best of ways, because I'm so thankful for the quality time.

Knowing how meaningful it is to my kids, because I took the time to be curious about how I can improve, it's the most valuable work I can do. I wanted extreme results. I wanted to be a better father because I knew I wasn't doing it right, and I had to ask the question that Kevin asked. Even though the question related to products and businesses, the application to both my business practices and my family was priceless:

What was the problem, and how could I get to that magical transformation?

I could ask them to tell me what was wrong, then shut up and listen.

Curiosity leads to questions. Asking the right questions gives you invaluable information.

But what to do once you've gotten it?

Kevin knew how to get focused and make a plan—and he had plenty more to teach me.

CHAPTER FOUR

GET FOCUSED AND MAKE A PLAN

So many entrepreneurs believe they get stuck because they don't have an adequate plan.

In Kevin Harrington's world, they don't get stuck because they don't have a plan that's good enough—it's because they don't have a "perfect plan." And they never will.

"There's no such thing as a perfect plan," Kevin told me on a trip to New York from Chicago. "If you strive for a perfect plan, then you are most certainly going to fail. If you're striving for perfection, you've gone twenty percent past where you actually needed to be to figure out how to get the right plan in the first place."

75 TO 80 PERCENT

"How do you mean?" I asked him.

"Remember what I told you about procrastinating perfectionists? That you only have to get an idea to the seventy-five to eighty percent level, and then you need to deploy it? There's more to it. You *have* to embrace this concept, because the odds are so overwhelmingly stacked in favor of the idea that you've got something wrong. There's only one way to find that out. Act. You have to act on your ideas.

"The truth is, without a lot of formal training, most entrepreneurs are fairly decent at taking an idea to the seventy-five to eighty percent level. We all know someone—maybe even ourselves—who has a natural instinct to think through certain elements of an idea or opportunity to get to that level. It's almost human nature. What *isn't* instinctive is that ability to pull the trigger and act without it being perfect.

"The instinct is to do the opposite. Once we get closer to the end of our planning process, that's when we have to actually *do* something with it, or we have to get feedback about it, or we have to put it out into the marketplace. That is where all the anxiety and fear soaks in. That is where the entrepreneur says, 'I'm not quite ready. I need to keep planning. There's more to do.' I've lost count of the number of people I know who got to eighty percent and stalled for *years*."

He was right. There was a gentleman we brought in through the Ziglar program who had his idea at the 80 percent level for four years before he met us. *Four years*. It took meeting us to push him into action. What he learned in the following four months was likely 10x what he learned and discovered in those four years of planning.

It's why Kevin doesn't believe in the five-year business plan.

"Six months," Kevin said. "Once you take something to eighty percent and deploy, you're going to need to pivot so many times through that early implementation that it would be impossible to see out any further than half a year. The only kinds of companies that can plan five years out are your Procter & Gambles of the world. They're 100-year-old companies with a long history. They have the luxury of thinking five years ahead.

"Not entrepreneurs. Entrepreneurs need to be looking at a six-month time frame for a business plan. Period."

He was right. As soon as he said it, I realized that I had been looking too far out. I have to admit, though, that it took me some time to fully embrace the concept, because initially I thought that it meant everything had to be on a six-month time frame, including things like the budget. However, that's not what he meant. It's still important to have cash-flow projections for the year and have your financials in order. It's the planning that shouldn't stretch beyond that half-year mark.

It's not something Kevin just prescribes offhand—it's not lip service. Even as of the writing of this book, in some of the ventures we are currently involved in together, we don't look past six months in our plan, because we know when the end of that time period comes, we'll be adjusting all over again.

This doesn't just hold true if you're just starting out. Say you have an existing business. In that existing business, your sales and structure can be planned further out. If you were to come up with a new idea for a product, or a new sales channel or a new division? You guessed it—you should still go back to that six-month planning window for anything new that you're trying to develop or implement.

One of the main reasons why this is so important for entrepreneurs and not large, established companies with a long history is that entrepreneurs, for the most part, are wired for the pivot. We are wired to have many failures and to recover from those failures. Big companies pride themselves on *not* failing because they've done so much research and development with the notion that most of their ideas succeed. The degree to which they succeed can vary, of course, but they tend to have very few failures.

Entrepreneurs can and will fail a lot. In fact, as you'll see, this has been and always will be a core theme for Kevin. Are you going to rise stronger than you were when you failed? Are you going to fail fast? If so, then how can you really look that far in advance?

A Blank Canvas

Kevin and I have made several business trips to Brazil. On one such trip, Kevin delivered a speech about his nine steps to business planning. What I learned watching him there was that because of his aggressive curiosity, Kevin is constantly open to change and learning.

One of the ways that Kevin used to plan was a brainstorming method, similar to whiteboarding, but he'd use sticky notes. He'd essentially place a SWOT (strengths, weaknesses, opportunities, threats) analysis on the sticky notes—what is the opportunity, what is the marketplace like, what are the problems? He'd stick these notes all over the wall and move them around as needed.

He would essentially create his business plan in this way. Sometimes he'd remove a sticky once he discovered the information was irrelevant. Sometimes he'd add to a daisy chain of sticky notes. It was more of a rapid planning process versus formalized strategic planning that has a long process of discovery, research, and development.

As a result of sharing this tactic, someone at the speech—someone who was there to learn from Kevin—introduced him to the idea of canvas brainstorming or planning. When Kevin learned what it was, he loved it so much, he offered to pay the gentleman for his idea.

The man's name was Alexander Osterwalder, and he wrote the book *Business Model Generation*.

The concept behind the book is there are nine segments, or nine building blocks that any company—especially a new one—needs to think about in terms of launching their business so that they can accelerate the process.

Using a whiteboard, or even Kevin's sticky notes, you look at nine straightforward areas:

1. *Who are your key partners?* What are the motivations of those partners and the partnerships?

2. *What are the key activities of the business idea?* What key activities does your value proposition for your business require?

3. *What are you going to deliver to the customer?*

4. *What problem are you solving?*

5. *What is your relationship to the customer?* What relationship can you expect to establish with them, and what will be the cost of that relationship?

6. *What class of customer are you targeting?* What's your target segment, and what's your avatar?

7. *What key resources does this business or product require?*

8. *What distribution channels are required for this product or idea to get to market, and what is the cost?*

9. *What is your main revenue stream?* How are you going to sell this to customers, and how are they going to pay?

"I loved the idea of the canvas," Kevin said. "To me, entrepreneurs are, in some ways, like artists. They sit down at this blank canvas, which to some people, represents an impossibility. They say, 'There's no way I can fill this empty space. I can never do this. I've got to work for someone else. This is not for me.'

"To the entrepreneur, though? The blank canvas represents endless possibilities. They say, 'The world is at my fingertips. All I need is a good idea.' Then *boom*, they can start taking themselves through these building blocks.

"They say to themselves, 'I just need some key partners who can do these key things. I need the right value proposition, and then I need key customers in these channels. If I have the right resources and distribution channels, and I can get the cost to this level, then I'm going to change the world.'

"The canvas idea was so appealing because it was so simple. It took what I was doing with the sticky notes and simplified it even more. It put a word picture to what I was already doing in my life in real time. I love simple.

"For example, whenever I run into a problem, I love to use the fishbone model for problem solving.

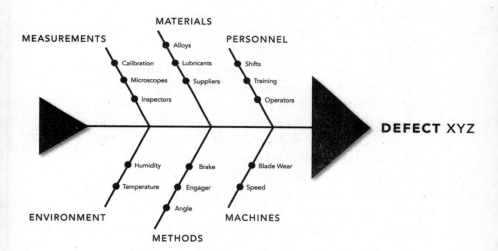

"The *problem* is the 'head' of the fish. Then you draw a line from left to right. You draw slanted lines along that line that represent the 'bones' of the fish. On those lines, you write what the *causes* of the problem are and their source, such as sales, production, or employees. It's a super simple diagram that allows you to concretely visualize an issue instead of just talking about it abstractly."

How I Was Getting It Wrong

We go with what we know.

Before I met Kevin, I was engaging in strategic planning. I learned it from my time in corporate America, working for companies like Kellogg's and *USA Today*. *USA Today* is owned by Gannett, which is to say it is *highly* influenced by a very large corporate structure. At the time, I believe Gannett owned up to 50 newspapers. Suffice it to say, they were huge. Kellogg's was more than 100 years old. They'd been strategic planning for years.

Those processes were what I knew, and though as an entrepreneur I found them to be challenging and ineffective, I didn't believe there was an alternative. I didn't realize that by the time I finished my strategic planning as an entrepreneur, I was already behind. I'd already had to pivot three times, so my plan was obsolete, and I wouldn't use it, which would put me in the worst of all situations. Not only was my plan no longer the necessary one, I was left with no plan at all.

It became an all too common reality to face. I found myself, like many entrepreneurs, simply going off my guts and trusting my instincts without any plan whatsoever. I looked at guys like Kevin Harrington and just assumed he had the Midas touch—that he just came up with big ideas and ran with them because he knew they were good ideas. It never occurred to me that he was sitting down with a six-month planning process or some other simple form of modeling.

I had no plans. I had no models.

Zig Ziglar's son, Tom Ziglar, once said to me:

"The process takes the pressure off the person."

That simple phrase defined exactly what I saw in Kevin when I began working with him.

"The fishbone process," Kevin said, "the canvas business modeling, they are examples of these micro-entrepreneurial processes that can be used to flesh out whether or not an opportunity has good potential, or, if and when you face a problem inside of the opportunity, they help you to pivot and adjust.

"Those processes take the pressure off the person, because it gives them something to lean on when things go wrong. If you have no process to fall back on, fear becomes part of the equation. You're filled with all this anxiety and pressure. You tell yourself you're going to fail and go bankrupt. You quit your job to make more money, and now you're faced with these problems you never anticipated. It sends you into panic mode."

Kevin lives these processes, along with the notion of getting to 80 percent and planning no more than six months out. Then he duplicates them over and over again, and it takes the pressure off of any business or idea he engages with.

When it comes to that idea of duplication, would I had known then what I know now—although in some ways, in getting it wrong, I stumbled upon his methods in my own way.

"Can That Be Duplicated?"

One of the things I've found quite incredible about Kevin is the things he teaches me in retrospect. To share this story, we've got to go backward in my life to a time before I ever met Kevin in order to look at some of my earlier experiences through the lens of Kevin's mentorship.

One of my first businesses was one of the more successful ones I was involved in. Because it was doing well, we operated under the assumption that success would breed more success, when what we should have been doing was asking ourselves: *What was the process we used to be successful? Is it something that can be duplicated?*

We should have been asking ourselves this—but we didn't.

As we continued to bring in the cash, the bank eventually approached us—like they do—and told us that we could *really* grow the business if we had a line of credit. Of course, we agreed. In fact, we thought we could go crazy with this business—depending on how much we could get. We were a debt-free company at the time, making between $300,000 and $400,000 a year. So we asked how much we could be approved for.

The bank came back to us with an approval for a million-dollar line of credit—and we jumped on it.

All we needed was more money to double or triple our business, right? We had some significant success and access to a whole lot of capital. Once that money was in hand, we went to work launching a variety of new products, without a process and without a plan.

We woke up a year later doing the same amount of sales and a million dollars in debt.

We had exhausted our capital and done nothing to increase our revenue. That meant we had a huge nut to cover every month with a monthly interest rate to pay, and we weren't bringing in any additional money.

Clearly, we had a huge problem to solve.

Now, while this situation predates my time with Kevin, I saw in looking back that I employed strategies that he espouses to this day. In doing so, I've been able to draw further lessons from that experience by seeing them through his mentorship, whereas had I not had that, what happened might not have been nearly as impactful to me as it is today.

We sat ourselves down and said, "What problems does our customer have that we can solve?" Initially, we thought all we had to do was create and produce the product, and the people would buy it. The reality was that there were a lot of products out there, but there were very few people solving problems.

The business was a manufacturing one, and we sold to retailers, but prior to that, we had been retailers ourselves. We got into the manufacturing side because retail had been problematic for us, and no one was solving that problem. The issue we encountered was when we went to trade shows and bought a product, and that product didn't sell, the manufacturer still expected to be paid. The only way we could recoup our money was to clearance that product.

As a result, our entire profit for the year did not have to do with the good products we picked—it had much more to do with our ability to get out of the bad purchase decisions we had made. Said another way, our profit was largely tied up in "clearancing." Many think that when they see retailers selling items at 50 to 75 percent off that they're losing money on their product when, in fact, getting that money is how they keep the revenue they made on their full-price goods. Take any apparel retailer—they've likely made incredible profits on their high-ticket items, but it's all sitting in the inventory of bad decisions they made. They can't realize their revenue until they've gotten rid of those items.

That was the problem we had as retailers, so we started a company based around solving it—not just for us, but for all. Our method was to guarantee the sale of the product so that the retailer would never get stuck with something they couldn't sell. We had a really clever way of helping the product move so that the retailers could always make full margins on anything they bought from us. It was a brilliant idea, and it was why we were so successful.

Then we got all this money.

With it, we decided that all we had to do was come out with more products. In doing so, we walked away from solving a problem and simply started producing. The minute we abandoned that original notion, we were on a path to put ourselves $1 million in debt.

Fortunately, we discovered quite quickly that it was departing from our original goal of problem solving that put us in this situation. We relaunched ourselves with the tag line:

"At Cottage Garden, we take the risk out of retail."

We quadrupled down on the idea of solving that problem and made sure every product we made aligned with that goal. With that pivot, the next thing we knew, 24 months later, we had not only paid off our line of credit, but we'd made a million dollars on top of that.

As I said, Kevin wasn't in my life at this point. However, I can look back at that experience through the frame he established for me to see how we were able to accomplish that turnaround—by leaning into duplicatable processes proven to work that we could replicate over and over again. We determined the problem and the causes in a concrete way that let us work definitively toward solving them. We didn't overstrategize. Once we knew what we needed to do, we acted—and we did so to great success.

Reflecting on that story, I realized the value of Kevin's mentorship to an even greater degree. It drives home the whole idea of having a process you can lean into—one that you can replicate time and time again. That's how you scale a business, and how you can ensure your success as an entrepreneur.

Where Kevin's guidance has really come into play is my understanding that if your processes are simple and strong enough, they can apply to nearly every business.

Including the business of my family.

FAILING TO PLAN . . .

Kids—and their parents—can get some grandiose ideas in their heads, much like entrepreneurs.

The kids decide one day that they want to backpack across Europe or that they want to climb Mount Everest. The parents, on the other hand, say they want their child to go to Harvard, or that their son is going to be a professional soccer player.

How can you hope to achieve any of those lofty goals without a plan? Remember, the flaw I realized in my family is that we weren't even purposeful enough to sit down and have meetings about what we wanted to accomplish. It's a sure bet other families are making that same mistake.

Families, for the most part, just don't plan—we didn't. They don't plan to be successful, and even when they do, it's more for these elaborate things like Everest and Harvard. There's no canvas planning and brainstorming.

Due to Kevin's mentorship, when it came to my children, I decided that if they had an idea, we would plan—but just up to 80 percent. Then I encouraged them to act on it.

My daughter Grace told me that she loved to help others. "I want to be a missionary in Africa and help needy kids there for the rest of my life," she told me.

"Okay," I said. "But how do we back that up a bit? What are some things we can do around here *first* that would help other people?"

Next thing you know, we're brainstorming, and we came up with an idea. In our community, there is a food bank where needy families go. It takes volunteers to operate it, to pass the food out and get it from the trucks. My daughter was hesitant at first.

"I don't know anybody there," she said.

"You want to help these children in Africa," I said. "You feel it's what you've been called to do. Let's start with something local—something you can act on *now* and see where that takes us."

Grace began volunteering at the food bank. Through that work, she found out that she could help needy families in Indianapolis, so she volunteered for a program that goes there to help. That one program turned into several others. She ended up getting on the philanthropy committee in our county.

Kevin and I had donated to the building of a school in Africa and took a trip there to visit and to help build. I took my eldest daughter, Mary, with us as Grace wasn't old enough to make the trip. While doing this work, she noticed that most of the kids there didn't have shoes. They were making them out of smashed Coke cans that they turned into sandals, or they would tie pieces of other shoes together to put on their feet—or they simply wore nothing at all.

Mary came back and shared this with Grace, who now had the experience of duplicating much smaller successes in helping others. As a result, she saw herself as being able to take things to the next level toward her goal of being a missionary in Africa.

"You know what I'm going to do?" she said. "I'm going to collect shoes for those kids, and I'm going to set up a collection station in my school."

We sat down and did our own canvas planning. It wasn't perfect—at all—but we got it to about 75 percent, and she deployed. She set up a collection depot at her school, a huge box covered in white paper with the name of her endeavor, Shoes for Change. The goal was to get kids at her local school who had extra pairs of shoes that they weren't using to put them in the box. The white paper was so they could sign their names on the outside after they donated so that she could take that with her to Africa along with the shoes when she had enough to justify the trip.

It worked, but not enough to generate enough shoes. One school, one box, one idea was not going to be sufficient to put shoes on all the feet of the kids in this orphanage she found in Nairobi, Kenya. She started making phone calls and found out that other schools in the county would be willing to put these boxes there as well. Suddenly, she had three schools with three boxes, and word got out. She called *every school in the county,* unsure of who would say yes or no.

The next thing we knew, there were collection depots in *every school in the county.* She ended up on the front page of the local newspaper. They did an entire feature on Grace and Shoes for Change, and in a span of a few weeks, she collected more than 1,500 pairs of shoes for *five* orphanages in Africa. She even raised the $2,000 to cover the freight and shipping to get the shoes there.

Make no mistake—Grace is not planning to be an entrepreneur. However, she has benefitted and is changing the world because of the entrepreneurial lessons I learned from Kevin Harrington and brought home to the business of my family. If I had chosen not to share what Kevin had taught me, this goal that she had never would have been realized—not because she doesn't have a huge philanthropic heart and not because kids didn't need shoes, but because I would have essentially robbed her of this opportunity had I chosen not to share what Kevin had taught me.

Grace is now well on her way to becoming a missionary in Africa, and she will change the world. As of the writing of this book, she was accepted into a summer program at Harvard Medical School. She wants to be a pediatrician for the villages in Africa that she served with the Shoes for Change program. Someday, families from those same villages will call her "Dr. Gracie."

If Shoes for Change had just remained an idea, forever in the planning stage, the chances that this might have come to pass were slim to none. Shoes for Change is now in the process of becoming a 501(c)(3) nonprofit foundation that will live, hopefully, beyond Gracie. Because she acted on an imperfect plan, she has already left her legacy.

Taking that kind of decisive action, however, to some might seem easier said than done. In the next chapter, we'll dive a little deeper into how Kevin taught me—and therefore my business and my family—about how to do so with confidence.

CHAPTER FIVE

TAKE ACTION

I fell victim to something that many entrepreneurs commonly do—inaction. Before I tell you all about how, let me explain how this happens to people like us.

Kevin and I were once speaking about a business venture, and in the middle of the conversation he said:

"I learned early on that sometimes you've got to start a lot of fires before you find the one that's burning the brightest."

FEED THE RIGHT FIRE

What he meant was that he is always looking for new business ideas that will be a hit, but that will hit at a 100x multiple. To do that, as he'd said before, you can't sit back and over-plan. You have to act on those ideas—start the fire, see which one burns the brightest, and then pour gasoline on that one. You've read that in these pages before, but it bears repeating, until it becomes a mantra of sorts.

It's also important to understand that you just can't do it once.

A great number of people think Kevin is a business genius because of the success he's had. The truth is that he understands the odds and is willing to lean into them. He's also willing to have nine failures in order to get to that one 100x success. In order to do that, immediate action is required. He has disciplined himself not to over-plan. By over-planning, you can actually make yourself fail slowly.

Now to some, this idea might seem counterintuitive. How can planning cause failure in this way? Overstrategizing, putting in place an elaborate plan, doesn't prevent failure—in fact you're more likely to do it at a pace that costs you far more in the long run than if you had failed quickly, as Kevin is wont to do.

Kevin always wants to fail fast. If it's going to be a bad idea—if the fire is not going to stay lit, then put it out. Don't artificially keep it going just because you're willing it to succeed when it's not meant to.

I participate in a communications thread as part of masterminds. (If you've never attended or heard of a mastermind, it is a fairly exclusive community of successful entrepreneurs and mentors who work together with the end goal of assisting each other to achieve their business goals.) In it, I saw another entrepreneur post this elaborate plan for a new business idea they had. Part of this plan included spending $100,000 on Facebook advertising, not to obtain leads or sales, but simply to push out the idea and build a following around and for it.

Someone in the thread spoke up to serve as the voice of reason and asked why this entrepreneur didn't just start by sending an e-mail to their list to see if there was any actual interest in this offering. It was a valid question.

Here this person was, willing to spend $100K to build this community around their concept before they even knew if anyone was interested in it. As it turns out, this person had a list of more than 6,000 people. With that large a number, they could have put together a seed launch, send it out to those thousands of people, and gauged their interest before they spent dime one on advertising.

Unfortunately, this idea of spending and elaborate planning is typical of today's entrepreneurs. They embark on these long journeys of strategy before they ever actually prove the concept. Then they're so invested that they'll keep going, even if it's a bad idea. They'll keep feeding that fire.

If you test an idea and people like it, you don't need all that extra planning. You've validated the concept, and now you're ready to spend the money and go all in. It's not about knowing when you have a *bad* idea—it's more about knowing when it's a *good* idea. If I put something out there and nobody raises their hand to say, "I want more of that," that's not scalable. Spending $100,000 on that makes it 100,000 times harder to walk away from it. You blind yourself to the truth. It's the greatest entrepreneurial trap.

And I fell right into it.

Back when I was in the manufacturing business, we created a product line called Mary's Moments, named for one of my daughters. It was a line of paper products—journals, note cards, and gift sets—and it was very successful.

We also have a son named Markus, and we were feeling guilty that we had created a line named for our daughter but not for our son. We created a second company called Markus, a frame and décor line.

It turned out to be a complete bomb.

It was simply a bad idea—but because we put our names on it, we willed it to be successful, and it just never was. It became a huge money pit. We couldn't abandon it when we should have because, in some sense, it felt like abandoning our child.

As entrepreneurs, we tend to put on blinders we didn't have when we had our initial idea, and then we don't act quickly enough to test it to see if it's actually a good idea. In my case, what we should have done was taken the concept for the Markus frame and décor line and showed it to our sales reps, getting their opinion before we ever created the line, bought the product, and tried to sell it.

We put those blinders on because we made it personal. We took it way, *way* past its usefulness and lost a great deal of money on it. Mary's Moments was done very organically. We had an idea and the marketplace loved it. We didn't set out to create this hugely successful line. Instead, we acted on the idea in a small way. We took the idea to the market, and they validated it—*then* we scaled it up.

We didn't use that same thinking with our son's line because we made the mistake of thinking it would just work out the same, so we developed the entire line and came out with it all at once, making it far harder to shut it down and walk away. We kept the fire burning for three seasons—a year and a half—and it shouldn't have lasted one. We tried to retool it and come out with a different version but to no avail. Three seasons in the manufacturing world is a long time for a product line that was unsuccessful from day one.

There were so many reasons it went wrong. There was a ton of competition in the market. The price point wasn't quite right. It wasn't unique enough a product.

Perhaps most importantly, it wasn't our core competency as a company.

Mary's Moments focused on paper goods—stationery, note paper that sat on a desk in a pop-up frame, note cards in a special carrying case. The Markus line was all around jeweled, fabric, and wooden photo frames. Mary's line received instant reception. Markus's did not.

"You can't create these elaborate plans and then put blinders on about when it's time to pull the plug," Kevin said, when I shared this story with him. "You should be looking for people to raise their hands to tell you, 'I want this,' long before you get too far in the planning. The last thing you want to do is try to convince the market that it's their fault that they don't want it. You have to look to light fires that burn on their own fuel—not ones you have to keep feeding to keep them from burning out.

"Let them burn out, because you'll discover *why* they burned out—although sometimes you don't need to know. Sometimes you just have to accept that they did. It's one of the hardest parts of being an entrepreneur because we get so invested in our ideas."

The irony, though, is that together, Kevin and I had a difficult time following our own advice. After listening to him, I told myself I'd never make that mistake again—except I did. And he was right beside me in it.

AN EXCEPTION TO EVERY RULE

I've talked about the fact that Zig Ziglar was a mentor to both me and Kevin. When we got together on the project designed to bring his teachings to a new generation, it became apparent fairly quickly that this was a fire that needed to be put out. It simply wasn't getting the results we wanted.

However, because he was our mentor and because he impacted us so significantly, we pursued it, counter to our own philosophy, and it never became what we wanted it to become. Granted, we likely wouldn't have had the relationship that we do now had we not gone after it, so good things came from the endeavor in that sense. Because of our love for Zig, however, we overinvested in it.

Yet with any rule, there are exceptions.

If you get to a point where you've had some success and you decide to do something because the world needs it done, then there might be cause to break the rules. You might elaborately plan and overinvest in an idea if the reason you're doing it serves the greater good—if it initiates some change you want to see in the world. You can't go all-in on a mission or cause, however, if you need that cause to put food on your table and provide for your family.

Kevin and I were driving to extend the legacy of a mentor that meant so much to both of us. We were not driven to make this a multimillion-dollar entity. We were not driven to make this Kevin's next $100-million business. We did, however, overinvest—but neither of us looks back on it with one ounce of regret, because in essence, we were paying it forward. We were giving to another generation what we had been given. Kevin wanted this for his children—so that his sons, Brian and Nick, and his grandchildren would have the opportunity to know and love a mentor of his.

Therein lies a situation in which you can break that rule. It can't be with your last dollars—you can't cash in your 401(k) to extend the legacy of a mentor.

The good news is that from the perspective of extending Zig's legacy, the endeavor was quite successful. Tens to hundreds of thousands of people now have access to the Zig Ziglar brand—so many more than if we had never done it.

We continued to invest because the outcome was matching our objective. That's why it's so important to recognize that sometimes there are exceptions to the rule—that you can invest in something simply because you're passionate about it, because the satisfaction from that can pale in comparison to what the world views as success.

ACT NOW IN ACTION

Politics aside, there is no better example of Kevin's ability to take action than the story of him and Donald Trump.

"I had these salespeople working for straight commission," Kevin told me. "I would take them to trade shows and say, 'Let's find some products here.' We'd find some, and then I told them, 'Let's get some celebrities attached to these products, because by itself, that Chinese wok might not sell.' At that time, we were starting to deal with the Jack LaLannes and George Foremans of the world. My sales team pushed back."

"'Kevin, how are you going to get these people?' they said. I told them that I could get to anyone I wanted within seven days."

"Seven days?" I said to Kevin.

"Seven days," he answered. "I told them to give me a challenge. They told me to get to Donald Trump face-to-face in seven days. This was around 1987, right when *The Art of the Deal* came out and long before he'd become the forty-fifth president of the United States. I started with his secretary, because that was the natural first step. She asked what I wanted to talk to him about, and before I could finish the sentence, she said, 'Sorry, he's busy,' and hung up. So, I had to get creative.

"Tony Schwartz wrote the book with Trump and was much easier to get on the phone. I called him up and said, 'Tony, you don't know me, but I'm in this As Seen on TV space. I've got a question for you. If I needed a million copies of your book and was willing to pay for them, could I get a good wholesale price?

"His first response was, 'What was that?' I told him that I might need a million copies of *The Art of the Deal*, but I needed the best wholesale price he could give me. He asked who I was and what did I do. I told him that I sell products on TV that help people make money in real estate. My thought was that we could offer Trump's book as an upsell to the people we were talking to at the time.

"'Do you really think you could move them?' he asked. Again, I told him I'd need a great price, along with Trump's approval, but I was confident that I could move hundreds of thousands, maybe millions of books.

"'Let me call you back,' he said. Two hours later, he does call me back and says, 'When can you come to New York and meet with Donald?' I was in his office three days later. I drove there from Philadelphia."

It was the epitome of taking action—not elaborately planning. Not a dime of money put down. Kevin's story didn't stop there.

"So, there I was in Trump Tower. I got off the elevator and his secretary was right there, seated outside his office. From behind the door, I could hear him screaming at someone about gold versus silver. Yelling and shouting for a good twenty minutes. The secretary was looking at me like, 'Good luck, pal.' Finally, he shouted, 'Where is that kid that's got something to pitch me? Get him in here right now!' The secretary and I looked at each other again and I went in.

"The first thing I did was reach for the chair to take a seat. Trump said, 'Wait a minute. Don't sit down. You're here to pitch me something, and I don't even know what it is. Before you even start, if I were to say yes to your pitch, how much of my time are you going to need, and what's my upside? Because if you don't have the right answer, you're going to turn around and get the hell out of my office.'

"So it was put up or shut up time. I said, 'If you said yes to my proposal, I'd need maybe three to four hours of your time and you could make four million dollars.' I came up with it quickly because I knew it had to be good. Short time, big money. He waited about five seconds. Then he said, 'Okay, sit down.'

"We spent an hour together. My basic pitch to him was that we would use him in an infomercial to sell real estate opportunities. I actually walked out of the door with a handshake."

By the time they got to the lawyers and everything else, the deal never happened. Trump didn't want to actually appear in the infomercial. He thought Kevin just wanted to sell his content. But the point is that Kevin didn't have an elaborate plan when he ended up in front of Trump. He didn't even have an elaborate plan to get that meeting. He took action. The end result was beyond his control, but his ability to keep fear of failure from putting him in a state of "analysis paralysis" put him in Trump's office.

SUCCESS OR CONFIDENCE—WHICH COMES FIRST?

So many entrepreneurs—and people in general—believe that you have to be confident to successfully take action.

But is action the chicken or the egg?

Kevin will tell you it's the egg—that it is the *action* that creates confidence, not the confidence that creates the action.

He believes the same thing when it comes to motivation. People believe that you have to be motivated before you take action. Kevin believes that taking action fuels your motivation to then take the next step instead of taking more precious time to think and plan. It's in those moment that your confidence and motivation are negatively impacted.

Kevin once told me that you are far more likely to act yourself into feeling than feel yourself into action.

Our mutual mentor Zig Ziglar said:

"If you're standing there, listening to me, trying to figure out how big a step you can take, it's probably too big, and you're not going to take it. So here's the deal: I don't care how big of a step you take. Take whatever size step you can. But do it right now."

As always, Kevin had a perfect story to share with me to illustrate this concept.

"There was a television network in Saudi Arabia called Arab Radio and Television Network, or ART. They had five channels that all went dark at midnight and came back on the air at six A.M.—thirty hours of unused airtime!

"The owner of ART was a billionaire sheik named Saleh Kamel. I met his people at a trade show, and after talking for a bit, they told me that they would love to have me come pitch the sheik and tell him why he should do business with me.

"You have to remember that this was in the early '90s. I was a young entrepreneur. I hadn't had anywhere near the success I have today. Said another away, I was terrified.

Here I was, going from a trade show to flying thousands of miles to pitch a billionaire sheik, who, by the way, controlled the bureau you had to go through to get a driver's license there!

"I was nervous beyond belief. But I leaned on the teachings of Zig, particularly his ideas around using a person's fear of loss as a negotiation tool and decided I would go make my pitch. I actually took Zig's book with me on the trip. I knew that the sheik was a sophisticated businessman and that if I went into that meeting showing any kind of lack of confidence, any deal I might make would be dead in the water.

"As with the Trump meeting, he was already quite busy when I arrived. When I got in front of him, I said, 'Mr. Sheik Saleh Kamel, sir, I really appreciate your time, but I'm not going to sit in this chair to present my opportunity until I disclose something to you. It's very important that I do this. I want you to know that I have been in discussions with your competitor, Orbit, that also has some channels here in the Arabic nations. I don't want us to go through hours of meetings only to have you find out that I've been talking to them, so I wanted to tell you up front.'"

My mind was blown. Here Kevin was, in the office of someone who stood to give him one of his biggest deals to date at that time, and he was telling him he was already talking to someone *else* about the deal. Talk about confidence!

"So, the sheik said, 'Wait a minute. Orbit doesn't have the money I have, and I have five channels.' Then he turned to his assistant and told her to bring his son into the room. When he arrived, the sheik said, 'Tell Mr.

Harrington how powerful we are and why we are better than Orbit.'"

My eyes went wide. "So, the sheik was pitching *you*?"

Kevin smiled. "The sheik was pitching me. I spent the next two hours getting his pitch about why *I* should do business with *him*. He was not prepared to lose out on a deal to Orbit. He took me out on his one-hundred-fifty-foot yacht and on a tour of his multiple mansions. He had me as a guest in his home. I started out with a thirty-minute appointment and spent three days there. In the end, we walked away with a twenty-five-million-dollar commitment. He financed the whole deal, and I didn't have to do one bit of selling.

"Just imagine what I would have missed out on if I had given in to my nerves and my fear and not taken action. If I had told myself that I wasn't successful enough to meet with the sheik, let alone tell him I'd been meeting with one of his competitors. Taking action in that way only gave me more confidence, and it resulted in one hell of a deal."

BRINGING IT HOME

The idea of taking action has undoubtedly impacted me more than any other lesson Kevin has imparted to me. It obviously changed my view and perspective on business.

However, it also dramatically changed my interactions with my children. It made me take pause and say that I wanted to weave this into the fabric of who they were. I wanted them to be action takers. I didn't want them to be held back by fear of failure. I want them to try a lot of things. I want them to start a lot of their own fires.

When my daughter Grace was in Africa, she met a young man named Edwin who suffered from the same severe scoliosis that she did. We were fortunate enough to provide Grace with the surgery she needed to correct her painful condition, but Edwin was not so lucky—and Grace, with her philanthropic heart, could not abide this. She could not live with the thought that she could have this procedure and he couldn't.

"I can't just pray for him to have that surgery," she said.

"What are you going to do about it?" I asked her.

"I have to act," she said.

You can see why she makes me—and now Kevin—so proud.

On the third day after her own surgery, Grace went to work creating a GoFundMe page to raise the exact amount of money Edwin needed to have the procedure.

We instilled in her what Zig Ziglar had instilled in us, and what Kevin's experience had driven home for me— quite literally. It didn't matter how big a step Grace took to raise what would seem an insurmountable amount of money for some young boy she barely knew. What mattered is she took that first step, and she took it immediately.

On the GoFundMe page, she wrote her story and Edwin's. It raised a little bit of money, but not nearly enough. I told her that while she had my complete support, I was not going to be the dad that gave her an anonymous donation to cover the rest, and to her credit, she never wanted that. However, suddenly, we saw the donations pick up in frequency, seemingly out of nowhere.

About two weeks in, I was at a mastermind event. A few attendees had seen Grace's post on social media and donated. They told me that they had gotten the most incredible letter from Grace after doing so—that the letter was so amazing that they had shared it with all of their friends and family. It turns out that to every person who donated, Grace wrote lengthy, personal thank-you letters that ended with asking people to share her and Edwin's stories with their community.

We only knew the first 10 people who donated. After that? Strangers with kind hearts who had been contacted by people who were touched by the sincerity of her words and sympathized with her and Edwin's situations.

Had this 15-year-old girl elaborately planned how to raise $9,700, two things would have likely occurred. She would have gotten frustrated with the whole process and cast it aside; or she would have strategized and strategized, failed, and would have been devastated at the result.

But we had Zig Ziglar. We had Kevin Harrington.

Grace took action. She took that first step, and the first people who donated gave her the confidence and motivation to keep going—not the other way around. The first act gave her the momentum to push forward, to write those beautiful letters, and to achieve her ultimate goal—and she did.

She needed $9,700. Three weeks after beginning this endeavor, she raised $9,815.

Grace not only felt her way into action—she acted her way into feeling.

And what a feeling.

Six months after the campaign ended, I was at a business dinner in Florida, and somehow Grace came up. Someone sitting four seats away said, "What did your daughter do?" As it turned out, that person had been at an event the month Grace launched her GoFundMe, and the keynote speaker—whom I had never met or heard of—put her picture and her page on the main screen as an example that age does not limit you from taking action and helping others. I was able to share the rest of her story:

how her campaign caught fire and finished funding in just 21 total days.

FROM THE ASHES

We've talked a great deal about failure in this chapter. The truth is it's inevitable.

The other truth is it's absolutely necessary—and it needs to happen quickly.

At another event I attended with Kevin, I learned just how much Kevin has failed in his career. The answer might surprise you.

You'll also be surprised to learn how integral it was to his success.

CHAPTER SIX

FROM FAILURE TO PHOENIX

Kevin taught me that failure is part of the process. It's something that you have to embrace. However, he doesn't set the expectation that you should fail on purpose. Nobody ever sets out to fail—Kevin least of all.

Fail Fast . . . but Not on Purpose

What Kevin does want to do is fail fast, and fail cheap. He doesn't want to spend a lot of money when he fails. He wants to learn from the failure, adjust, and pivot. While he doesn't look to do this on purpose, he does accept the fact that failure is largely inevitable for any kind of entrepreneur.

"I tend to get frustrated with entrepreneurs when I've invested in their company, or even when I'm just helping them out," Kevin said, "when instead of measuring twice

83

to cut once, they're measuring ten, fifteen, and twenty times. And then they never cut. Just like taking action. They overthink to the point where they never do it.

"I've seen that the reason that they do this is because entrepreneurs are a passionate bunch. They believe they've got a great idea, and their DNA is wrapped up in it. They personally identify with their product or venture. So if the product is a failure, they see themselves as a failure. For a lot of these guys, that's a hard pill to swallow. But if they're going to be successful, they have to find a way to do that.

"They need to think of themselves as a phoenix. Embrace the idea of rising from a failure stronger than you were before you failed. The phoenix is a mythical bird that repeatedly rises from the ashes of the burning of its past self. In entrepreneurial terms, the ashes of your predecessor is the failure of your business.

"The only way a phoenix gets stronger is that the previous version of itself has to die. The previous version of yourself is this idea, dream, or desire that you have."

If you can fail and rise stronger? Then you're on the same path as Kevin Harrington, along with many other extraordinary entrepreneurs.

I was attending an event where Kevin was speaking, not far removed from the time of the writing of this book. There were a number of up-and-coming entrepreneurs there, and Kevin spoke about his incredible journey. When it came time for questions, the people in attendance asked the usual questions. They wanted to know all about Tony Little's Ab Isolator and the Ginsu knives.

However, after Kevin had been speaking for a little more than an hour, someone in the audience finally asked a different question.

"Can you tell us about some of your failures?" they asked.

"You want to hear about my failures?" Kevin responded. "Do you have about five more hours?"

The crowd had a good laugh. It's true that Kevin has had multiple successes that have become part of our cultural vernacular—the Ginsu, the Gazelle, and a number of others that are instantly recognizable to us. What we don't know about are the literal hundreds and hundreds of products that failed on the way to giving us the products we now know and love. Kevin has taken 21 products to more than $100 million in sales.

But that was out of more than 500 that he launched.

THE CHUBBY CHECKER TWIST-A-SIZER

As the seminar continued along this line of questioning, someone asked Kevin:

"What was your greatest flop?"

Enter the Chubby Checker Twist-A-Sizer.

For you younger readers, Chubby Checker is a musician who popularized the dance craze "the twist" with his cover of the song of the same name in the 1960s. Further capitalizing on this cultural phenomenon, Chubby tied his name to an exercise product called the Twist-A-Sizer. Essentially, it was a machine that allowed you to "twist and move" in order to lose weight.

"I liked the idea and invested hundreds of thousands of dollars in it," Kevin said, "and it failed miserably. I lost a ton of money. The moral of the story is this: if someone comes into your office with a weight-loss product, and their name is Chubby, you might want to say no."

That's a bit more of a punch line than the actual moral of the story—though it's actually sound advice. What is important to take away here is that Kevin failed. He failed often, and he failed big.

"I'd be willing to bet," Kevin continued, "that I have failed more times than everyone in this entire room. That for all the success we've been talking about and celebrating here, that not only have I failed more than all of you here, I'd be willing to go on record and say I've failed more times than anyone you've ever met."

What was so remarkable about his sharing that story and that sentiment was how the audience leaned in to what he had to say. Sure, his incredible successes were fascinating to them, but in many ways, they can feel unattainable to most. In that moment, he humanized himself to the crowd, and it made them even more attentive to the lessons he'd learned on his journey. His talk had already been a home run up until that point. He could have easily rested on his successes and left them with a talk they'd ultimately already heard before.

Instead, he delivered an incredible truth—that if one measured success based on a failure-to-success ratio, Kevin was the biggest failure in the room.

However, he rose stronger from each failure. It's how he was able to go "from zero to hero" on so many of these products—how he was able to have so many $100 million successes.

I've learned in working with Kevin that there are three kinds of entrepreneurs: ones who fail and quit; ones who fail but grit it out and refuse to accept the failure, grinding away to their own detriment; and ones who accept that they've failed, take a step back to see why, and use the information to emerge new, improved, and stronger.

Kevin is clearly that third entrepreneur—but I had to know how he came to have this level of adaptability and resiliency, as it was obviously quite uncommon.

COMES BY IT HONESTLY

"Remember I told you that my father was a World War II hero," Kevin told me, "who flew in the Air Force. They literally flew 100 feet over the ground and dropped bombs. North Africa. Italy. He flew one hundred sixty-five missions in his time. Back then, you only had to fly twenty-five and you could go home, because the experience could destroy you as a person. The constant adrenaline wreaked havoc on you. You went out with ten guys and came back with five, because two turned back out of fear, claiming engine trouble, and the other three were killed in action, because eight men were fighting fifteen Messerschmitts.

"So, he'd done his twenty-five missions, but he stayed, and he got shot down twice. He was going so low to the ground that a pistol shot got his fuel tank. But even with that, there was no quit in him. He saw that there were kids coming in and getting picked out of the air like that. So he, along with Tom Sutton, another man who stayed in the Air Force with him, remained there to keep coaching these guys. They were the world's first coaches for flying the P-40. My father fostered such trust in Tom that Tom insisted my father marry his sister when they returned home. Tom was my Uncle Sut.

"The point was that he had to learn from every mission, and the ones that were failures, particularly the ones where he got shot down, were the ones he learned from the most. Most everyone would get out after their twenty-five missions, let alone after they'd been shot down twice in the same day. But my father took that information and not only learned from it, but also passed down that knowledge to the pilots that came after him. And he passed on that resiliency, that adaptability, to me."

Reading this book, you and I find ourselves in the fortunate position of those young pilots, learning from the best, as Kevin now passes on to us all that he's learned.

But as is typical of me, I didn't learn to appreciate it right away.

No Elevator—Only Stairs

When I started working with Kevin, we began a venture together called Xponential, Inc., where instead of having an actual product, Kevin Harrington was the product. That is to say, his brand would be. We would look for ways to leverage his brand to exponentially impact opportunities and ideas inside of that venture. For example, people would pay a fee and travel to Saint Petersburg to talk with Kevin about their business and learn from him how to craft the perfect pitch. Then Kevin would shoot a testimonial video for them. That video would exponentially impact their business and prove quite lucrative for us as well. It was created to live out his idea of multiplication by impacting the businesses of others that fit his brand.

So, there I was—I had just partnered with the original Shark from *Shark Tank*. It seemed everything he touched turned to gold, and he had decided to start a business with me. I was going to retire a multi-gazillionaire simply because we partnered together. Right?

Not exactly. We've been in business together with Xponential for just about three years as of the writing of this book, and it has taken the exact same cycle as almost every business Kevin has ever been in.

That is to say that the first ideas we had for Xponential did not succeed. They were not profitable. Of course, I thought it was me—that I was the fly in the ointment. It *had* to be me. How could it be Kevin? He had the Midas touch. The whole thing just started off a lot slower than I thought it would.

Not Kevin.

"To get our one big thing to hit," he said, "we're going to have to try ten things. This is no different from any other business I've ever been in. When we find the thing that hits, we'll double down and pour gas on that fire."

Of course, I didn't think that was going to be the case. I had partnered with Kevin Harrington! He had this whole "new business venture" down cold. We didn't need all these iterations. I thought he had this whole thing figured out—and he did.

Kevin understands so well that not everything is going to be successful and that you're going to have to adapt as a result. That this didn't take off like a shot was no shocker to him. He knows this so well, in fact, that as of this writing, we had the biggest month of revenue in the company's history. We adapted to the marketplace and found our niche in it. We're on the precipice of things blowing up and really taking off.

And we're on the tenth iteration of the business. He's scary good at this.

Zig Ziglar once said:

"There is no elevator to success. You have to take the stairs."

The truth of that statement not only applies to new entrepreneurs—it applies to Kevin Harrington. People assume that he never has to take the stairs, but I'm here to tell you that he does, especially on a new venture. Ours was a brand-new one, something he'd never done before, so there was no elevator for either of us. We weren't in the infomercial space where he already had traction. We weren't in the physical product space where we already had huge fires burning. We were taking on digital products and e-mail marketing, a space we hadn't previously explored. There was very little we could borrow from our other fires to start this one. Instead, we had to start our own group of them to find one that burned brightest.

Whether you're a new entrepreneur or you've got some experience in this game, take heart in this notion. Successful entrepreneurs are not successful all the time. When I partnered with Kevin, I got in the elevator, pushing all these different buttons, hoping it would take me right to the top. It was the equivalent of me saying I have a T-shirt to sell, and I know that the apparel market is a $100 billion market, so I'm instantly going to be successful because I have apparel to sell there.

That's just mashing buttons, hoping one takes you to the penthouse.

In the meantime, Kevin had already taken the first step on the stairs. When I realized the elevator wasn't going anywhere, I had to hop off and catch up to Kevin, who was already ahead of me by a couple of flights.

Xponential has been a terrific case study in adaptation, and it's because Kevin, once again, learned from the mistakes in his past to rise from the ashes.

THE AB ISOLATOR

I'm going to venture a guess that a good deal of you have heard of Tony Little and some of his exercise products. One of his huge hits was the Ab Isolator. What most people don't know is that the first time out of the gate, it failed.

"It wasn't because people didn't buy it," Kevin told me. "They did. The problem came when they received it and saw that it was literally a nylon strap with a little bar for your feet—and they returned it. The return rate was through the roof because the perceived value of what they paid didn't match the product they got.

"Now, most of us would see that as a straight-up failure. We'd tell ourselves that a product with this kind of return rate just wasn't going to work. But I realized that our problem was not our ability to sell—it was our ability to match the value expectation of the customer.

"What we did was we went and recorded all of these trainings about how to use the Ab Isolator—fitness training to show customers how to use it to get better abs. At the time, we could produce CDs on the cheap, so we created this set of six CDs that would come with the Ab Isolator. Even if you didn't think the Isolator itself was worth much, the trainings carried the value expectation. We could have fit all of the trainings on one CD, but we put one routine per CD because the cost was so low, which felt like it had even more value to the customer.

"The Ab Isolator went on to do three hundred fifty million dollars in sales.

"By all rights it was a failure, and a disastrous one. The business was built on keeping return rates low, and ours were so severe that we were losing money on every show we were doing. We adapted and pivoted to increase the perceived value, and it took off to become this massive success.

"That success bred success. Because of what happened with the Ab Isolator, Tony Little became his own name brand. That enabled us to come out with a little product you might remember called the Gazelle."

"I remember that," I told him.

"You should, because off the success of the Isolator and Tony's brand, the Gazelle did a billion dollars worldwide."

My jaw fell open.

Here Kevin had what was, by all rights, a catastrophic failure with the Ab Isolator. Not only did that pivot garner them huge financial success, but they effectively turned Tony Little into a household name, which converted into mega success with the Gazelle. None of this would have occurred without that first failure.

A phoenix from the ashes.

"What Does This Make Possible?"

Helicopter parenting is a big problem today. We never want our children to fail, and we'll do almost anything to prevent it from happening. In doing so, we are allowing them to take that elevator to top, only to have them find out later that, in the real world, there is no elevator to success. We don't allow our children to take the stairs, neglecting the fact that we won't be around forever to pick them up when they fall, or to keep them from falling altogether. When they have to climb the stairs themselves, their legs don't have the strength.

I say "we" because I did this, too.

But because we approach our family life as the business of family, we have adapted Kevin's philosophy to our unit. My wife and I now want our children to experience failure because that's where the growth is—in the struggle.

The story of the butterfly is the best example for this. If you break open a butterfly's cocoon, you leave it unable to fly away. It must push through the chrysalis to remove the gunk from its wings and to develop the strength necessary to take flight. When we take on the role of the helicopter parent, we are breaking open the cocoon for our children, and then we're scratching our heads as to why they can't fly on their own, when the answer is so painfully obvious.

With Mary, my eldest daughter, I was putting her on the elevator every chance I got, opening the cocoon whenever I could. Kevin's philosophy of the phoenix made me realize that I was hurting her—not helping her. I saw quite clearly that there was little she could do without my help.

I recall very specifically a time when she needed my help with a paper for school. In the past, I'd help her do a great deal of the research. I told myself that this time would be different. I told her I would only help her with some of the typing, or I would offer to read and edit after she was done.

To say she offered some pushback is kind. When I placed the yellow "caution" tape on the outside of the elevator and declared it out of order, that was not a fun time for Mary and Dad. The transition to taking the stairs was a rough one.

But, man, was it worth it.

Mary needed my help less and less. She only used me to help her brainstorm ideas for her papers, and then she was off to the races. Over the course of a few years of being allowed to struggle—and more importantly, fail—she developed a terrific independence. By the time she was a senior in high school, she applied to 30 colleges on her own—and she got accepted to every single one.

She was not the number one kid in her class. She wasn't valedictorian or salutatorian. She just worked hard and learned from her struggles and failures.

So much so that she applied and won a full scholarship to her number one choice—worth $200,000. That never would have happened if I had continued to take her up the elevator.

Mary wasn't my only phoenix.

My son Markus spent over a year preparing to go to China. His plan was to study Mandarin there and train in the martial arts. He had to go through a number of hoops and hurdles to achieve this, many set up by us, because we didn't want to make it easy on him. He had to get ahead in his classes, he had to study some Mandarin ahead of time, and he had to maintain a certain GPA. He did all of that—so he got to go. While there, he had a terrific time. He loved every minute of it.

And then he did something that was—quite frankly—dumb.

He was out with a group of guys, and they started throwing rocks. Markus ended up smashing his fingers and had to be taken to the hospital. It was quite an ordeal. The end result was his being kicked out of the martial arts school because he could no longer participate.

That school was also where he was studying Mandarin.

All of his work, all of his efforts, came crashing down under the weight of one bad decision. I had to fly over to China to bring him home.

Markus was devastated.

"Markus," I said, "this is bad. I know you're heartbroken and disappointed. This was everything you wanted to do, and you were having a terrific time. But now I want you to ask yourself, What does this make possible?"

He couldn't go back to school in the States because the semester was already halfway through. As a result, he had a period of a couple months where he didn't have anything. So we decided that what this incident made possible was that he could travel with me on my business trips until school started again in the fall.

We went to Jeff Walker's Product Launch Formula conference, as well as Ask Live with Ryan Levesque. We flew to Brazil together, where, for the first time in his life, he got to speak on stage—and with me. I'd never spoken on stage with any of my children.

All of these conferences, all of these mastermind events, ended up changing his life forever.

By traveling with me, Markus got the chance to meet all these extraordinary people, and he had passions stirred within him. He became passionate about becoming an entrepreneur. He became passionate about becoming a pilot—so much so that he joined the United States Air Force. Even while in the Air Force, he's been engaging in entrepreneurial activities, learning real estate.

Far and away, he is not the same kid as he was at that moment in China. He's become more disciplined and responsible, particularly because he traced back losing that opportunity in China to a lack of both qualities.

By all rights, Markus would tell you that that incident was one of his greatest failures.

He could have moped around the house, sitting in his room for two months. Instead, because we instilled in him the lessons I gleaned from Kevin about failure, those two months turned into an intense and incredible opportunity for him. It changed his view of the world by giving him the chance to see even more of it. He even traveled with me through his senior year, missing 36 days of that school year—every one of them worth missing for what he gained.

When he looked back on it, he said to me:

"Look what I might have missed had I not failed there. Look what I did next as a result of my failure. Look what it made possible."

Fathers don't have moments much prouder than these—and I have Kevin to thank for it.

I also have Kevin to thank for teaching me a new kind of math when it came to success—both in business and in family.

He taught me how to stop adding—and start multiplying. I'll tell you how in the next chapter.

CHAPTER SEVEN

MULTIPLY YOUR EFFORTS

The best image I can give you to help you understand Kevin's extraordinary exponential thinking is this:

The man does not have a plus sign on any calculator in his home. He only thinks and works in terms of multiplication.

I can sit with people and talk with them about Kevin for 30 minutes or more, and no statement resonates with them quite like that one. For Kevin, if it—whatever "it" might be—if it doesn't multiply, then he's not interested.

When you adjust your mind to this way of thinking, and you look out into a sea of opportunities and ventures, you no longer see them in a linear sense. You don't look at them in an additive way. Multiplication is about exponential growth, and if you can modify your brain to think exponentially, you'll separate yourself from a large

contingent of entrepreneurs. Exponential thinking separates the goods from the greats.

We've always heard that geniuses see the world in a
way that is different than anybody else sees it. Consider the
early web adopters and what they did with e-commerce and
search engines. When they looked at the world, they saw it
in the way that we now experience it today.

The genius entrepreneurs—geniuses like Kevin—see
it as their calling in life to multiply. Kevin doesn't only
want to multiply his business endeavors. He wants to multiply his relationships. He wants to multiply his time. Two
becomes four, four becomes eight, and so on. He always
looks for 100x opportunities, because 10x opportunities
can be achieved linearly. 100x results would take a lifetime
to achieve if you only thought in terms of addition. If you
multiply, 100x is simply 10 times 10.

To reinforce this idea, Kevin told me about when he
started the small business network.

"I was introducing people to franchise opportunities,"
he said. "If people chose to become involved with that
franchise, I was then paid a commission. It was great, but
it was a linear model, because this was all done one person
at a time. I had to make my thinking exponential.

"I said to myself, *Wait a minute. I'm spending all of this
time making a pitch, and then the franchise turns around and
does the same thing once I connect the prospect to them. What
if we can just do this really well once, and then tap into some
kind of national network that exponentially distributes it?*"

It was from that question that the infomercial was
born. It arose out of Kevin's desire to go from linear to
exponential results.

He was getting terrific results one buyer at a time. The
franchise was, too. Nobody was unhappy with what was

happening. When a sale happened, it was a good one—but if the franchisee only had to do one really great presentation, then those sales would exponentially accelerate.

Enter Arnold Morris and the Ginsu knife.

"I was at the Philly Home Show when I saw Arnold cutting through a Coca-Cola can with one of his knives," Kevin told me. "I went to the home shows, the hardware shows, and the fitness shows. This came from my father's mentoring. Despite the fact that he had his restaurant and worked eighty hours a week, he had all these side ventures, because he always said somewhere in those, you're going to find exactly what you want for yourself.

"So at the show, I see Arnold, and he's delivering this eighteen-minute pitch to an audience gathered around his table, around fifteen to twenty people at the most. I should mention that his close rate for that group was really good—but when those fifteen people were gone, guess what? He had to get another group of them to gather around to do it again.

"The plus side of this was that he absolutely perfected his presentation. But it was all linear. So I said, What if I filmed this once and put it into an exponential distribution system? Would people react to it the way those fifteen people standing around his booth did?

"I presented the idea to Arnold, and he was in. The thing was, I didn't have much money at the time. I had to figure out a way to film it that was affordable but that still looked good. We ended up filming in the back of a grocery store because they had an area that had knives and gave us the look and feel we needed. I hired a film crew to come in on a budget of two thousand dollars.

"Arnold nails it on the first take. He'd done this presentation thousands and thousands of times already. It was short and tight. Still, I always liked multiple takes on these kinds of things, just in case people come up with a better way of saying things on the second or third try. We do it another time, and Arnold repeats his first go-round down to the word and gesture. It was incredible. At that point I said, 'Yeah, we're done. This is good to go.'

"That one presentation where Arnold was making money off of fifteen people at a time at state fairs and trade shows? That we filmed in the back of a grocery store for two thousand dollars? That pitch went on to do five hundred million in sales."

The Arnold Morris story blows me away to this day. It is the ultimate example of exponential thinking. Here was a man who was selling his widget or problem-solving product to however many people he could gather around his table, and then he was selling it to the world. Best of all, the *same* amount of effort went into selling to fifteen people as it did to generating $500 million in sales—the exact same presentation. Nothing changed. It was simply recorded and distributed exponentially.

Arnold would have never made that kind of impact had he continued on his linear trajectory. He spent decades on the state fair circuit and was away from his home 40 weeks a year. That was his life. It took Kevin, a multiplication seer and an exponential thinker, to pull Arnold out of that rat race.

"It's Who—Not How"

Dan Sullivan is a renowned coach, and he has a saying: "It's who—not how."

Exponential thinkers don't think in terms of how—they think in terms of who. I can validate that by asking this: of the more than 500 products that Kevin has launched in his lifetime, do you know how many of those products he created himself?

I'll tell you—not one.

The only product he actually created himself was an absolute bomb. In this sense, he is the ultimate example of "who, not how" because he doesn't go looking for the "hows." He doesn't search for *how* to solve a problem—he finds *who* has already solved it. Then he multiplies their problem solving with his ability to think and distribute exponentially. That's how nearly all of his success has been achieved.

Any given person can grow linearly. They can become more efficient. They can shave off a few minutes from a task here, a few hours there—but those are linear results. All of those add to what *one* person can do. In order to multiply, you must bring other people or other variables to the equation. So many entrepreneurs believe that they can't multiply their efforts because it's just them—and in some ways, they're right. It *is* difficult to do by yourself. Kevin would teach me how you bring others into the fold later in our relationship—and I'll share it with you, too.

The first step, however, is to get rid of plus signs in your life and learn to see the multiplication signs.

On another one of our trips together, Kevin told me a terrific story about his work with an app developer who wanted to get a million downloads.

"StarShop was an idea that I had," Kevin said, "where we would put an app on a mobile phone and get celebrities on it so they could sell their products. Kim Kardashian, 50 Cent, you name it.

"It was a mobile app, which meant we needed to get it on mobile phones. The traditional way of getting people to download an app is to market it—to make customers aware of it. But that's a long road to a million downloads. It occurred to me that the way to multiply our efforts, and quickly, was to go to one of the mobile phone companies and partner with them so that they would *include* the app on all of their phones.

"I got a meeting with Marcelo Claure at Sprint, and I laid a presentation on him. I told him that he sold a million cell phones a month, and if he put our app on there, we'd give him equity in it along with a percentage of all sales, and it would cost him nothing. He'd have all these celebrities telling their fans to go to that app.

"It was a twenty-minute meeting. At the end of those twenty minutes, he literally jumped out of his chair and said, 'That's an unbelievable idea. I love it.'

"It was just like when I saw unused space on the screen on Discovery. I'm looking at all these empty spaces on my phone screen just waiting to be filled by apps. Now, instead of taking the long route of advertising the app on Facebook and YouTube and what have you, now we've got the thing preinstalled on millions of phones. It took a couple of months to get the deal finalized, but when it was, Sprint launched StarShop on six million phones."

I saw the parallels to Arnold's story immediately. Arnold didn't have to change what he was selling to get $500 million. Kevin didn't have the app company do anything different with the app. He took both of them from a linear business model to an exponential one. He got them out of the mind frame of selling to one person at a time and into one of multiplying their efforts with the same product.

And he did this by leveraging other people's time, resources, and information.

TRANSFORMATIONAL—NOT TRANSACTIONAL

The secret to Kevin's success is a notion I discussed earlier in the book—the win-win relationship. Kevin does not establish transactional relationships, because they are typically a one-shot deal. You can have any number of transactional relationships. The fact that they're one-time doesn't mean that they can't be beneficial—but they're not set up to multiply. They're linear.

Kevin creates *transformational* relationships, ones that are scalable to infinity as long as each party wants to remain in them. A transformational relationship is exponential—it's when all parties involved use their 100x thinking, where all sides can say, "This deal is a win for me."

He does this by putting so much energy into striking a fair deal, as opposed to a generous deal or a "shark" deal. A generous deal is one he strikes with you because he likes you, but as time goes on and you start to scale, you find that this wasn't an investment from him in your business—it was a generous transaction that he provided, and he's no longer there to help you scale it. He offered that transaction up to help you out as an act of generosity—that one time.

My son is into motorcycles. If he buys one and gets an excellent deal, he'll come home, tell me all about it, and we'll high-five his good fortune. But if the guy that sold him that motorcycle has another customer come along and tell him, "I would have paid you a thousand dollars more for that bike," how do you think he's going to feel about that deal? My son Markus feels like he hit the lottery—the man who sold him the bike feels like he got taken. If Markus goes back to that same man to buy another motorcycle, the chance that he's going to be excited to give him another terrific deal are slim to none.

Entrepreneurs go through life looking for the best deal, which is a transactional exchange—and those can be great as long as they understand that those are one-time situations and not scalable.

Generosity is not scalable. Getting the best of someone is not scalable. It takes someone who is truly an exponential thinker—someone like Kevin—to understand and see that if they get too much out of this deal, the person on the other end won't want to do this deal with them again when it scales. This happens all the time. Most partnerships, most joint ventures, fall apart because one party or the other sees that one side is winning far more than the other. That's when the deal is over. We've said it before—that's why so many businesses fail to make it past $10 million—because they've structured deals early on that aren't scalable. In the worst cases, one partner sues another because they didn't get a fair deal.

Very few transformational deals get a "high five," where both parties are incredibly happy with the deal—the aforementioned win-win. That's important to know and remember. This is the case because each party involved has to give up that part of human nature that wants the best deal for themselves. You simply can't get the best deal for both of you and have that arrangement be transformational and scalable.

DON'T FISH IN YOUR OWN POND

"It's difficult to multiply in your own ecosystem," Kevin said, "but so many people tend to fish in the same pond that they came from. For example, Arnold Morris could have collaborated with other people who were selling like he was selling. The only thing that would have amounted to would have been him on the road an additional ten weeks a year, because those people would have just told him about more shows he could go to, or better shows, or what have you.

"And, look, his sales would have increased—but linearly. You've got to get out of your own ecosystem to be able to think and grow exponentially. We need diversity for creativity. It's why I read so many different newspapers and trade journals. Yet so many of us go against that grain. We only watch one news station. We only read one newspaper. We only check one app. We allow ourselves to become creatures of habit.

"I do the opposite. The journals and papers I read go across multiple platforms. If you're in my home, I've usually got a news station on low volume in the background feeding me information. I'm asking everyone I meet questions like I did when we were looking for holograms. My ecosystem didn't have the answers I needed, so I had to step outside it. I had to collaborate with others outside of my industry.

"Now, that's not to say you can't grow inside your ecosystem. Are there people in your industry doing things better than you? Of course! Can you grow incrementally? Sure, you can. It happens through efficiency. It happens by selling more or doing more with less time or fewer resources. There are businesses that are built on this type of linear improvement, and that works for them. But the best you can do inside your own ecosystem is 10x.

"I want 100x. I want to know what *other* industries, other people, other entrepreneurs are doing. For example, I'm a huge proponent of masterminds, because it curates people who want to grow and achieve, but who have diverse backgrounds, often from different industries.

There are masterminds that are also very niche, but those are for the people who want to improve inside their own industry. I seek out the masterminds that are broader in scope."

This concept resonated with me, because prior to meeting Kevin, I was quite guilty of fishing in my own pond. I certainly wasn't participating in masterminds. Now the exact opposite is true. As a result, I've been more readily able to leverage the time, resources, and information of others to my own benefit.

A perfect example? This book.

This book would not be published had I not had a mind-set shift from linear to exponential thinking. I held a very linear view of how books were done. The creation and production of this book is the ultimate example of investing in relationships and networks. As a result of attending masterminds, Kevin and I were multiplying by leveraging. The publishing deal came out of relationships we had formed outside of our industry. We didn't know books. We relied on people outside of our ecosystem to tell us how to do it, because the ones inside our ecosystem only knew how to reach a certain size audience with their books. We wanted to 100x that number.

Trust is a huge factor when it comes to forging these relationships. We found our publisher through networks, but we would only work with people we knew we could trust, based on recommendations from people we knew well.

"When I look back," Kevin said, "some of the most successful deals I've ever made have been done face-to-face with a handshake. A contract is a piece of paper that holds people accountable because it's a litigation element. It has nothing to do with trust. For the most part, the most scalable deals in my life were based on trust. Things change.

Life changes. Markets change. If you trust the person, then you've got unlimited possibilities. If your entire deal is based on a piece of paper because you don't trust that person, there's no scalability in that. There's no multiplication. That's a linear deal. There's nothing transformative happening there."

It's Gotta Be the Shoes

Remember Grace and her shoe project?

Grace came to me at one point and said, "Dad, how do I get my shoe boxes in more locations?" as she only had one in one location at that point. So I encouraged her to think exponentially.

"Isn't your Girl Scout troop a county troop?" I asked her.

"Yes," she said.

"And aren't there other schools in the county?" I asked.

"Yes," she answered.

"So, this becomes a matter of who, not how," I said. "What if you reach out to all of the principals of all the schools in your county and explain what you did here with your project and see what happens?"

She did, but it only worked for about half the schools. There were some principals in the county who never returned her e-mails—but Grace was not to be deterred. She jumped above the principals and went to the "who," which meant the superintendents—and it was incredibly effective. The superintendents not only returned her e-mails and got her into the schools that didn't respond, but they placed her shoe boxes throughout their entire school system.

It was Arnold Morris all over again.

Her initial thinking was "how do I get more kids in the school that I'm in to bring in more shoes"—but when she thought exponentially, she realized the answer was to put the boxes in more locations. Same product and concept—just multiplying the locations and number of students.

She took it even further.

At one point in time, I had met the president of TOMS Shoes, a $500 million shoe company that donates a pair of shoes for every pair sold. I was able to reach out to him and get Grace on the phone with his team that handled the charitable side of the business. They coached and taught her how she could get the shoes where they needed to go in Africa. Again—who, not how.

In Grace's case, her ecosystem was her family, but her family couldn't get more collection depots in the schools. She had to fish outside of her pond to get that done. She had to ask *who* could make this happen, not *how* she could make it happen. The how would have been linear. She was in control of how she could possibly get more shoes in the school she already went to, but that was the linear entrepreneurial way of thinking—"How do I sell more to the people I'm already selling to?"—versus "How do I duplicate in many places what's already working in one?"

My daughter Mary has a sugar glider business that started with her having one as a pet. A sugar glider is a very small marsupial, quite similar to a flying squirrel. They are a popular pet in the community of people who know about them. After Mary fell in love with that first one, she got a second. The two of them ended up having a baby, and she was able to sell it for $500. Mary has that entrepreneurial spirit in her, so she developed a relationship with the number one breeder of sugar gliders in the state of Indiana. The breeder mentored Mary when she saw this young lady wanted to have her own business.

In many ways, Mary would be a competitor to this woman—yet she saw the potential in my daughter and mentored her regardless. Mary bought a few more pairs of gliders from this woman. Not long after, she decided she wanted to retire, and Mary was in a position to buy her business from her. She did so and became the largest sugar glider breeder in the state.

Had she decided to simply keep acquiring a pair here and there and breeding them, I'm certain she could have grown her business linearly. By going to the largest breeder in the state and developing that relationship and that trust—setting up a win-win relationship and striking a fair deal—she significantly multiplied her success.

Developing relationships like these—ones built on trust—goes a long way in building what Kevin likes to call the "dream team." It's a phrase we've all heard before, but I would soon learn that Kevin has a unique insight into what exactly it means for—and to—him.

CHAPTER EIGHT

BUILD YOUR DREAM TEAM

I'd go so far as to say that the whole notion of a "dream team" might be one of the most important things I learned from Kevin. Once Kevin discovered that concept, he never let it go. His goal now is to always assemble a dream team around each business venture with which he's involved.

The idea of a dream team is nothing new. Everyone's heard of one, everyone says they want one, and no one needs to be convinced that they need one. However, invariably you get the same response from entrepreneurs when it comes time for them to assemble their dream team:

"I can't afford it. I can only hire or bring on to my team those whom I can afford."

So they compromise, adding to the team only those whose salaries they can manage. In doing so, they also compromise the whole idea of a dream team—or they don't assemble it at all—all because of that limiting belief.

That's at the heart of what I learned from Kevin—that the only thing that prevents you from having that dream team is yourself.

If you've got incredible funding in your business— you've done an IPO, and you're flush with cash—then you can go out and hire a dream team, no sweat, right? That's the most common thinking among entrepreneurs—that having an unlimited budget is the only way this can be achieved.

I'm here to tell you you're wrong—and I know because Kevin showed me how.

I've seen Kevin put dream teams together many times over, in most instances not paying them *anything*. He was able to sell people on the idea of the venture and the potential that existed in it, and they were willing to come on board and be a part of it.

Kevin told me that in order for him to be able to do that, a number of things need to happen.

"First," he said, "you must be open and willing *not* to own a hundred percent of the venture. The last time I checked, one hundred percent of zero is still zero. So many entrepreneurs fight so hard to hold on to this idea of their venture, but it never goes anywhere. When it's all said and done, they kept total control and multiplied it, and then the venture was over. For me, I'm happy to put a team together such that I can share in the equity or do a revenue share so that I can share in the success of the venture, but other people are going to make money as well."

The Arnold Morris story is a prime example of this line of thinking.

Once Arnold became this superstar juggernaut of the infomercials, Kevin invited him to be a part of his personal dream team. Arnold, who had had this terrific experience with Kevin, couldn't be a better testimonial to share with others like him. As such, every time Arnold went out on the sales circuit and someone came up to him with a product of their own that had infomercial potential, he recommended each and every one of them to Kevin.

Kevin didn't pay him a salary to be a part of this team. Instead, he told Arnold, "You make an introduction to me, and if we pick up the deal, I'll give you a percentage of the revenue."

As you can imagine, it wasn't long before Arnold was making more money from referrals to Kevin than he *ever* did from his own Ginsu knife program. In fact, it's possible to say that Arnold Morris was responsible for over a billion dollars' worth of business that Kevin did in his lifetime—again, above and beyond what he did with the knives.

All because Arnold was part of the dream team.

"I told Arnold," Kevin said, "that we were doing some good stuff together. That he probably knew more people like himself out there. If he thought we were doing a good job and if he believed in what we were doing, then I wanted him to come on board to be part of our dream team and start making introductions.

"There came a time, in the heyday of all of this, where the Ginsu knives had kind of run their course, and I had paid Arnold millions and millions of dollars in referral fees. Years went on, and Arnold's health started failing, to the point where he was literally on his deathbed. That's when I got a call from Arnold's wife.

"She says, 'Kevin, I'm so sorry to bother you. I know you're busy. Can Arnold have just a moment of your time?'

"Now I'm thinking, okay, he's dying. He's about to pass. He's dying, and he just wants to say good-bye. So I'm steeling myself for this last conversation. Of course I say yes, and she puts the phone up to Arnold's ear. There's a pause. Then I hear Arnold's weak and cracking voice coming over the line.

"He says, 'Kevin, I've got one more deal for you. This one is a winner.'"

Can you imagine that?

It was Kevin's last conversation with the man. He passed a few days later. From the time they met to the time he took his last breath, that man was bringing deals to Kevin. He so loved being a part of his dream team that he never stopped looking for the next big thing, because he knew it meant something special for *all* of them.

When Kevin's infomercials really took off, Kevin put another team of people together. One of the clients he worked with had a product that was a huge success, so much so that his share of the deal was more than a million dollars per month. Kevin's accountant wasn't having it. He told him there was no way he could pay this man that kind of money. Remember, this was more than 30 years ago—a million dollars then was at least five million now. The accountant told Kevin he was doing all the work, and that all this man had done was to make the pitch. Kevin was buying all the media and taking all the risk. In his mind, there was no way that it was responsible business to hand over that million.

Kevin told the accountant to give him the check.

"I told him," Kevin said, "that not only were we going to give this man a million dollars, but I was going to fly to him and hand it to him myself."

That, my friends, is how you inspire loyalty. That is how you build a lasting dream team. That's how you get the reputation for taking care of your people.

Now? People clamor to be a part of Kevin's dream team.

DON'T HIRE WHO YOU CAN AFFORD

There are a thousand ways to hire someone, and only one of them is to pay them a salary. There can be profit shares in combination with salary. You can offer percentages of revenue or equity. Too many people out there have this limiting belief that they can only hire who they can afford, and that's just not true. It holds so many entrepreneurs back from achieving their full potential. If I'm scaling a business, I would rather have a hundred-million-dollar CFO for 10 hours per week than a million-dollar CFO for 60 hours per week.

When I say a "million-dollar CFO" I mean a CFO who has managed a million dollars. The CFO who has managed a million dollars is *never* going to get me to a hundred million. Never. Now, I might be able to pay the same salary to a CFO who can get my company to a hundred million, but I can only get him for 10 hours a week. That's okay, because he can get me where I need to go. The million-dollar CFO can work an unlimited number of hours, and chances are great that he won't get me where I need to be. He lacks the wisdom, the experience, the relationships, and the know-how to scale me.

Kevin knew that. He understood that because he figured it out early on in his career. He told me how on another one of our trips together.

"I got involved in a beauty product," Kevin said, "one that had a chance to be *massive*—but I needed to go out and raise a bunch of money. Of course, when you're raising money, people want to know that you have the right leadership in place, so they don't lose their shirts. L'Oréal was one of the best-known beauty products out there at the time—and I actually knew the president of L'Oréal North America through a friend.

"I was able to get ahold of him and told him about the deal. He told me he wanted a lot of money to come in on the deal. I told him, 'Okay, here's the deal. I don't have it, and I need to raise ten million dollars all told. I think we can get that done fairly quickly, and once we do, you will be well compensated.'

"Believe it or not, he jumped at the opportunity. He believed in the concept, and he knew I wasn't devaluing him, because what would most people do when they're presented with that kind of response? They'd negotiate, right? They'd say, 'I don't have all the money. Will you take less? Will you take anything?'

"Instead, I told him that he was worth every penny of the money he wanted. I wanted him to know that, in fact, he was worth more than that, but if he helped me raise that ten million, his money was going to be there. It got him excited, but it also ensured that he went out and did the work we needed him to do. He got so excited for the deal that he ended up bringing the former CFO of L'Oréal North America with him.

"We structured a separate deal for him. So now we're out raising money with the former president and former CFO of L'Oréal North America. We raised the money, and I never had to pay them a penny until the job was done. Talk about the ultimate dream team. Without them, there's a better-than-average chance we never would have raised that money at all."

Had Kevin hired who he could have afforded at the time? He might have gotten the front office manager at L'Oréal headquarters—maybe the bookkeeper. I don't mean that to be insulting, but that's who he could afford then. But because he was creative, he put his dream team together, got the funding he needed, and paid them what they wanted. Not a dime was spent until they accomplished their common goal.

The truth is that most entrepreneurs are bootstrappers.

If you've got a million dollars lying around to start a business, you've already had some success, you've already had some failures, and you know the difference between the two. As such, you have some idea as to how to scale.

The bootstrap entrepreneur gets stuck in the mentality of doing everything on a shoestring, such that when it comes time to put a team together, they're trying to do it as cheaply as possible. No one has taught them the lesson that they don't get who they can afford—assemble your dream team and get creative to create that win-win situation.

The surest way to *not* grow? Hire only who you can afford.

If you hire for where you *are* as opposed to where you're *going*, you will *never* scale to your potential. What ends up happening, once you've realized you've done this all wrong, is that you see you've spent a great deal of money getting to that first million dollars—and you've spent it on the wrong people. Once you understand that those people can't take you to *10* million, you know you have to change those people out, and that becomes an expensive proposition. There's drama. Before you know it, the business has lost its momentum, and it's struggling.

It's why it's much easier to get to a million than 10 million. One-million-dollar entrepreneurs hire one-million-dollar teams. It seems oversimplified, but it's true. Kevin has played this out over and over again, with L'Oréal being one of the best examples.

And it radically changed the way I thought about building *my* teams.

GIVE UP THE POINTS

I don't think in terms of sharing salary anymore. I work very hard to share profit. My mind-set around ownership is completely different.

Prior to meeting Kevin, however, I was the poster child for the entrepreneurial problem. I drank the same Kool-Aid as every other entrepreneur—I thought I was the only one who could own the business.

Working with Kevin, I realized that as the 100-percent owner, I was limited. I handicapped myself to having a dream team. I had to share in the opportunity for ownership to get the dream team I wanted in place. In order to do that, I started being open to having partnerships and revenue sharing—not just salaries.

What it's done for me has been incredible.

I've always had a knack for hiring well. However, it doesn't matter how well you hire—there's nothing like giving someone skin in the game. An owner thinks and acts differently—they have a different commitment that exceeds their talent and skill.

I believe we're wired that way. As human beings—particularly as Americans—we want to own things. We have a desire to possess. I travel to a number of countries regularly. In so many other places, people don't care if they own their home. It's simply not a big deal to them. They rent, and when they want to change it up, they change. They don't get caught up in the notion of owning their home. In America, we have to own it. It goes back to the earliest days of our history, when settlers went out west where it was nothing but snakes and wild animals, but they could own a piece of land.

If we know we're wired this way, why wouldn't we tap into that? Why wouldn't we leverage that as entrepreneurs to take things to the next level, to acquire better talent, to incentivize our people?

Of course, as owners, we feel we put our blood, sweat, and tears into our businesses, and we don't want to give that away. Realize, though, that ownership isn't something you have to give away immediately. When Kevin does this, people have to earn it. Certain markers have to be hit. Certain goals achieved. The L'Oréal story exemplifies this concept beautifully.

It kills me when I watch *Shark Tank* and I see people get the deal they want, but they're separated by a few points of equity, and the deal doesn't happen. It blows my mind. The benefit they'd gain by giving up those couple of points would far outweigh what they'd earn if they didn't, but they struggle mightily with giving up a piece of their company.

Plenty of my businesses failed. Learning what I have from Kevin, I'd much rather have a dream team in place that's just as vested as I am. I might put up the capital, but my team puts in their time, energy, and effort—time away from their family, putting in the extra hours. It creates extraordinary value for them and me.

As of the writing of this book, I started an e-commerce venture, and I hired an aggressive and sharp young lady to come in and help me. All along, I had her pegged as someone who would be an owner with me, but I wanted to see that she loved what she was doing and that she would do it well.

She did a *phenomenal* job. I sat her down and asked her how she'd like the opportunity to own up to 10 percent of the venture. She was over the moon. Of course, to get to 10 percent, she had to help the company achieve something—in this case, $100 million in sales. I'm giving her one percent for the first million, one percent for the next $4 million, and then one percent for every $5 million after that.

She was so happy and excited. It was like hitting the lottery. She wouldn't have been able to provide the financing to be a partner otherwise. I bring my wisdom, experience, and money to the table. She brings her talent and her drive and puts in the hours. It's the perfect combination.

How could I possibly lose in that deal? When all is said and done, this is likely going to be one of the most successful ventures I've ever been involved in, and I'm going to end up putting in the least amount of time in it. Not only was this a matter of "who, not how," but I found my dream team partner by giving up that precious ownership.

And it's all thanks to Kevin's mentorship.

THE FAMILY DREAM TEAM

When it came time to do things as a family, we started tapping into our children's unique skill sets and talents— their different interests and leadership abilities—to head up some of our family initiatives.

We found that our youngest child, Grace, was the most organized and detailed of all our kids.

So we would tap her to organize a task or activity for the family; and very quickly, the rest of the family, instead of being put off by the fact that she was the youngest, was glad not to have that responsibility. Even though Grace lacks some of the natural leadership Markus has, she makes up for it with an incredible discipline toward organization and structure. In fact, that allows Markus to lead more effectively because his sister makes sure that the details are covered and the task is organized.

The difference between families that think they are a dream team and those that actually operate as one is whether or not they are comfortable letting the right members step up to do the things they're uniquely wired to do. When that happens, the family can be extraordinary at so many things because the right people are in place to get things done. Odds are, it won't be the same person every time, and because of that, each person in the family feels valued because they get their shot to do what it is they're good at—which sets them up for success.

Families don't often take the time to figure out their uniqueness. I don't know many families that take the StrengthsFinder test. I definitely don't know any that take the DiSC personality profile. Yet many times, we wouldn't think of running our businesses without running our team through the Myers-Briggs, or whatever the flavor of the day is. Many employers won't even hire until candidates have taken that test.

Why aren't we using that same thinking at home?

Every family has the opportunity to be a dream team. It's a matter of finding out if they are willing to figure out what everyone's unique abilities are, what their unique skills are, and then approach tasks and challenges with the idea of who, not how.

If there's one thing I could do differently when it comes to this concept, it's that I would have labeled my family as a dream team much earlier. When I learned this from Kevin, I was already losing kids to college. If I have one regret, it's that I didn't plant the seed that God gave us a dream team when he put this family together. Even though I got pretty good at leaning into the strengths of my kids, I'm doing it with my adult children more now than

I ever did in the past because I understand their strengths more and can help them set themselves up for success.

Better late than never—because we're not done. Our team is still on the field. They may be spread out into different places, but we still have the opportunity to impact each other and lean into our strengths, even though we no longer share the same household.

I hope that if you are an entrepreneur with a family, you read this and realize that while you might begin building your dream team in business, you've already been gifted the *ultimate* dream team. You just have to lean into it, label it, and love it.

THE EXECUTIVE DREAM TEAM

I'm so proud to share with you in this book that Kevin now considers me a part of his dream team. When he has a business venture, he has me in the back of his mind thinking that it might be a good one for me to look at—that he wants to bring me in on the idea. In fact, Kevin has now established his executive dream team—me, his son, and two entrepreneurial attorneys. Now for every business venture he engages in, he involves one or more of us, but never all of us. He doesn't begin any ventures alone unless someone is hiring him for a specific speaking engagement with a singular fee. Even then, if there's some possible upsell or other extra element, he'll bring one of us in to handle it and share the revenue.

He's done this for me because he's seen me embrace his mentorship—the notions of:

▲ Getting the right mind-set

▲ Being aggressively curious

- ▲ Getting focused and making a plan
- ▲ Taking action
- ▲ Rising from the ashes of failure
- ▲ Multiplying, not adding
- ▲ Building the dream team

He's also seen how I've integrated all of the concepts to get scale—in everything. I'll tell you how in the next chapter.

CHAPTER NINE

GET SCALE (IN EVERYTHING)

Scale is the holy grail of the entrepreneurial journey.

Anyone can start a business. Anyone can make a sale or two—your mother can be your first customer. Your friends and family can make up the subscribers and followers on your social media accounts. It's not hard these days to do those things. It's not even that hard to begin to generate real business. It's not as easy to do it at a profit, but even then, it's not that difficult to experience some growth.

Growth is not scale.

Kevin and I know a business co-founder—someone we'll reveal at the end of the book—who discovered this. He would have liked to have had this realization sooner than he did, I imagine, but when he did, he did the only thing he could do to stop growing and start scaling.

He fired himself as the CEO.

GET OUT OF YOUR OWN WAY

As both the co-founder and the CEO, he could not scale his company. He simply was not meant to be the executive leadership of the business. It wasn't his strength. He was not utilizing his own talents and skills to the best of his ability, but because he couldn't let go of his baby, both he and his co-founder were limiting its ability to scale. Fortunately, through a series of events, they both had a moment of clarity, and they realized they had to get out of their own way.

So they let themselves go, brought in a new CEO, and put themselves in charge of departments that allow them to lean into what they're truly good at—and the company is flourishing. It is scaling at an unbelievable rate.

This happened not only because they got out of their own way. They also made the smart decision of keeping their business out of a red ocean.

BLUE OCEAN

Kevin taught me that if you truly want to scale, you've got to find some blue ocean.

"There are two bodies of water," Kevin said. "There's the red ocean, where everyone is in there killing everyone else. It's the competitive marketplace where everyone else already is. The water is red because everyone is at each other's throats, bleeding into the ocean.

"What you've got to get to, particularly when it comes to scale, is the blue ocean. Where is the water that isn't churning with competition?

"This concept isn't my own, but it's one I've adopted, and it has absolutely served me when it comes to scale.

It is difficult, almost impossible, to scale through a red ocean, because there are almost always huge sharks in the water. If you try to open up large discount retail physical stores, unless you're a *trillionaire*, you're going to have some problems. Walmart has pretty well carved out every piece of real estate in a market where it would make sense to do that.

"If you wanted to create and start an e-commerce marketplace right now, even though it's a massive business and Amazon is worth billions of dollars, unless you've got that kind of capital or are already well established in that space, you're not making a dent. Those are red oceans. You can take a swim, but it's going to be bloody.

"In the blue ocean, you can traverse waters quickly. You can scoop up a lot of customers and opportunities because the competition is sparse, or it isn't even there."

The Story of Daniel

Every once in a while, Kevin and I will hold events where people pay between $5,000 and $10,000 just for the privilege of sitting with Kevin. He talks to them about pitching ideas and imparts some of his wisdom—but in truth, people really pay that sum of money to pitch *him*.

We were at one of these events, and there were eight people sitting around a table. One gentleman named Daniel pulled an item out of his pocket and said to Kevin:

"I've got your next one-hundred-million-dollar idea."

What Daniel held looked like two tiny chopsticks, and when you pulled on one end, it had carbon fiber pads that went across a friction plate so that it ionically charged them. Their use? To clean your eyeglasses. The dust and dirt that collected on them would be attracted to the charged pads and when you put them back in the tube, they would recharge themselves. They were also designed with the edges just so to fit in the nooks and corners of your glasses. They were a great product. But Daniel was trying to go about things in a traditional sales route. He was approaching brick-and-mortar establishments, trying to sell it where people buy eyeglasses.

"I loved the product," Kevin said, "so I got involved. I told Daniel up front, though, that I didn't know how well this was going to scale inside a traditional retail model. However, I thought there was some blue ocean out there in the form of my access to television, demonstrated by my success with QVC and HSN. This product would fit perfectly there, because it was a demonstrative product. In other words, showing how it worked helped to sell it. Around the same time, Facebook was really coming on strong, and I thought it would be a perfect home to sell this thing.

"Nobody on QVC was selling something to clean eyeglasses. People weren't going to Facebook looking for how to keep their specs spotless. So that created blue ocean marketing channels for the product.

"We went to QVC first. They were slow to getting around to testing it for whatever reason, which left us scratching our collective heads for a minute. We knew we had this blue ocean market, but they didn't seem to want to move on it. Then they asked us, Can we create another item similar to this? Daniel also had another item that cleaned computer screens. Same concept. Carbon fiber pads crossing over a friction plate to charge them, but now at a higher price. Even with that, QVC passed.

"Here's the crazy thing: in the meantime, we took the original product to Facebook as we had planned. Come to find out, there were lot of people wearing glasses that were on Facebook, particularly from the older demographics. It took off like a shot, to the point where this little item the size of a miniature chopstick was selling thousands of units *a day*."

That's right. By the time this book is in your hands, this item has the potential to become yet another one of Kevin Harrington's $100-million products.

Not only that, but as a result of the success on Facebook, QVC, who originally turned it down, took notice. They then asked us to do a two-eyeglass-cleaner bundle with two separate colors. Kevin and Daniel agreed, and QVC tested it.

It tested so well that at their peak, they ordered hundreds of thousands of units.

It wasn't that Daniel wasn't growing—he was. However, Kevin added that "special sauce" that really helped him scale.

So, What Is Scale, and What Is Growth?

To use the language of the previous chapters, growing is linear. Scaling is exponential. Scale can't happen at a linear rate. Growth means you're seeing increases of 10 percent, 20 percent, maybe even 50 percent.

Scale is a hockey stick. You've got growth along the length of the hockey stick, moving upward at a slow but consistent pace. Then, all of a sudden, the stick curves up drastically, almost vertically.

That's scale. That's selling 15,000 units per day.

Consider a mom-and-pop restaurant that is successful and profitable. After a few years, they're able to open a second one. Those two restaurants do well, and after three or four years, they're able to open a third one. A few more successful years pass, and they open a fourth. They can continue growing in that model, and they can take 30 to 40 years to have a hundred restaurants.

Or—they can take their proven concept and reinvent themselves into a franchise. Now they can get to three *hundred* restaurants in the next five years if they want it.

That's scale. That's the end of the hockey stick.

The long part of the stick was starting the restaurant, making some money, proving the concept, and opening a second restaurant. It was linear growth. Franchising is what is scalable because they're using other people's energy, other people's resources, and other people's talents to duplicate what they've already done, but in a mass fashion.

However, let's be honest—we all know of some companies that missed their window to scale, and in doing so, failed altogether.

Blockbuster video was completely content with growth. They were growing every year, and they had the opportunity to buy Netflix for approximately $1 billion. That was their hockey-stick moment. They could have completely changed their business model, and for whatever reason, were unwilling to do it. Within a matter of years, not only were they no longer growing, they were bankrupt; and now Netflix is worth exponentially more than Blockbuster was at their highest value.

They couldn't—or wouldn't—get out of their own way.

THE PSYCHOLOGY OF PRICING

"When a person realizes that the price of their product is purely based on perceived value," Kevin told me, "they can value their product to the right audience.

"Sometimes we scare ourselves and say, 'Well, I can never sell my product for fifty dollars.' If that's what you're telling yourself, then you're not looking at it the right way. People have fifty dollars to spend all day long. What you really need to be asking yourself is, Can you get the perceived value to *exceed* the price? Because people don't make decisions to buy based on the price—it's all about their perception of the value of the product. People who scale understand this. If your price point is equal to your product or service's perceived value, that's not scalable. If you're *below* perceived value and price—well, that's a formula for not being in business much longer.

"The problem is, people often seek a match of perceived value and price. That's a growth strategy, not a scaling one. Scaling is getting perceived value above the price point."

Kevin was—and is—the master of this concept. Recall Tony Little and the Ab Isolator. It was successful, it was growing—but it wasn't scaling. It was a good item, not a great item, and so the price exceeded the perceived value. When they added those training CDs, the value skyrocketed and so did the sales.

"The trap you have to avoid, though," Kevin said, "is adding significantly to your own costs in the process of trying to increase perceived value. It doesn't matter if I increase the value to the consumer if I'm losing money on every sale. Tony had to go back in and record the trainings. That was a onetime expense. At that time, duplicating CDs cost cents—not dollars. A little bit of cost for a ton of perceived value."

It made perfect sense. There had to be some intelligence behind adding that value. The key, though, was to not let price be a limiting belief.

"One of the things that's worth so much money these days," Kevin continued, "is SaaS—software as a service. These companies are trading for massive values because they have figured out how to make one sale and then put their buyers on a continuity program, so they don't have to be resold every month. It just happens automatically.

"Amazon figured it out, too. There are certain items on there now that will cost, say $15, but if you agree to take the product every month, then it's only $13. It takes the same amount of effort for them. However, for the consumer, they've got to go to Amazon, log in to their account, search for the item, and so forth, every time they want to buy it. Or they can buy it once at that price point and never have to think about ordering it again because it happens automatically.

"These are the kinds of things that scale a business. Selling your product or service over and over again or selling it once and getting continuous revenue. Now every sale after that is exponentially more profitable and you don't have to build a whole infrastructure around it."

What separates Kevin from other successful serial entrepreneurs is the frequency at which he was able to scale ideas and businesses to that elusive $100 million. I mentioned earlier that he will be on his 21st such business by the time this book is in your hands. He's got a number of ventures doing so well now that it might even be 22— all because of his unique ability to scale.

For all of the great examples Kevin shared with me in regard to this, one of the most terrific stories came in the form of an energy drink company.

ENTER CELSIUS

Kevin loves energy drinks. He has one nearly every day. That's just who he is. Through his ability to network, Kevin ended up on the board of a small energy drink company based in Florida called Celsius. He loved their product, and it was a good one.

"They had research to show that their product actually helped people," Kevin said. "But, as with so many other companies, they were only growing. They couldn't figure out how to scale. They were getting limited distribution using food and beverage distributors to get them into retail locations, which was not and is not easy to do.

"In order to get that hockey stick effect, something radical was going to have to happen. A mutual friend of mine asked me if I had anything I was working on for Flo Rida. The light bulb went on in my head and I said: Celsius. I pitched it to the board, and they said run with it. I reached back out to my friend and said I was with a great company and we wanted to talk to Flo about an opportunity.

"We show up to his studio, with his brand-new Bugatti parked out front, and sit down with his manager. Flo's a buff guy, really fit, and he digs his energy drinks, too. I told his manager Flo would be the perfect pitch man for Celsius. He said, 'That's great, but he gets a million dollars just to show up somewhere.'

"Celsius was a start-up. In that early stage, they didn't have a million-dollar budget just for an endorsement. So I said, 'Got to be honest with you, you're thinking small. One million gets you what? Another Bugatti? Forget the million dollars. We will give you some shares of the stock. We're going to go out to the big food and beverage show, and you're going to put on a private concert for the top buyers there. Based on what we project in terms of volume, those shares will end up being worth far more than a million dollars.'

"Flo and his manager took the deal. He goes out to the show and puts on a killer performance for these top buyers. It was a small audience getting a private show from Flo Rida. It goes over so well that Celsius gets picked up by some the biggest companies in the industry with nationwide distribution. Over time the company grew to over three hundred fifty million in market-cap value and was trading for five dollars a share on the NASDAQ."

This wasn't a fly-by-night jump in stock value, either. At the time of this writing, Celsius was still trading at over $5 per share. Kevin is still on the board of directors to this day—and he's never sold a single share. He could have sold a long time ago, but he believes in the company. It was not a "pump and dump" scenario.

He sees good things in their future and will continue to be along for the ride.

WHSMITH

WHSmith is a British company that had retail stores in a number of locations, namely airports. Kevin shared another example of scaling with them—and me.

"So I'm sitting there with one of the top guys at WHSmith," Kevin said. "They're a hugely successful company. They had launched some television channels, and I had noticed that they had some downtime. I told them I had noticed—and their reaction wasn't quite what I expected.

"They said, 'We don't care that we have downtime. We don't like this American way of selling, these informercials that you do. They're too much of a hard sell. That's not going to go over here in England, and we're not interested.'

I don't mind telling you, they were a little rude about the whole thing."

"Something tells me that didn't stop you," I said to Kevin.

"Oh, no," he said, smiling. "I ran some numbers about how many homes they were in against the number of hours of downtime, and I came back to them with a proposal. I told them I was going to give them an up-front deposit, and I projected the income for the year to be equivalent to two hundred sixty-two of their stores in profit. They'd have no investments to make. We'd just be utilizing the downtime of their channel, so how would they like to have the profit of two hundred sixty-two stores without having to build anything or sign any leases?

"Of course, they were doubtful and asked how I was going to pull that off. Their airport stores averaged gross eight hundred thousand dollars, and they made one hundred sixty thousand in profit. I told them to multiply that by two hundred sixty-two, and that's how much money I'd give them for their downtime. I presented them with a five-hundred-thousand-dollar check and told them they'd earn six to eight million on it.

"When I put it in those terms, they were blown away. Now all of a sudden, that American way of selling wasn't so bad. They couldn't turn it down. They had a fiduciary responsibility to their board and their shareholders to say yes—and they did."

SCALING THE FAMILY

The bottom line of a family is not measured in dollars and cents. The growth of a family is not measured in top-line sales.

Four of my six children have now left the house. If I have equipped them—if I have prepared them for that next chapter of their life, then each of them represents a whole new entity, if you will. Scaling a family means answering whether or not the values and principles and things that matter most can transcend generations. Are your children able to have their own family and multiply what they've learned with you and integrate it into their children, and so on?

Having more kids is growth, not scaling. Having an exponential multiplier within a family can only happen when they start to move on and do their own things. What matters to our family is our reputation. That, to me, is the scalable element that exists within our unit. We have to ask ourselves if we passed on the core values that they will multiply not only within their own future families, but within other people in general.

Grace struggled most of her life to meet new people. It's hard to make an impact on anyone if you're afraid to even engage with them. The summer that Kevin and I embarked on this book journey, she made the decision to try to connect with more people. I told her that one of the best ways to do it was to ask questions. One thing people like to hear is their own voice, and one thing they love to talk about is themselves, so if you're interacting with someone, and they're talking more than you are, chances are they're really going to like you. It's a simple thing, but she deployed that tactic when she went to Washington, D.C., to attend the National FFA Washington Leadership Conference, where she ended up meeting so many people and impacting them.

"People don't care what you know until they know you care," I told her. The more she was able to listen and empathize, the more influence she found she carried with others. She now has the opportunity to impact so many more people than she once did—to share her thoughts and views and wisdom and worth with them, those values that we instilled in her. She is multiplying it out into the world. She is scaling our family.

More than scaling our family as a whole, though, what I learned from Kevin was how to scale my own relationship *with* my family.

I had a good relationship with my kids—but not a great one. I was growing that relationship, but I wasn't scaling it. I was parenting like everyone else—out of responsibility. I was taking them to school, showing up for their games, and asking them about their homework. If there was a bell curve that showed how much time the average parent spent with their kids, I was right there in the middle.

Yet I knew this wasn't the relationship I wanted to have with them. This is not what I dreamed of having when I imagined having kids. I had to ask myself how I could make this better. I couldn't quit my job to be at home more. Sure, I would scale my relationship with them, but then our family would go bankrupt.

What I landed on was the conscious decision to take one of my kids with me on every business trip I took. It removed the guilt of traveling so often, because I always had at least one of them with me. What I didn't realize is that the quality time I was spending with them sitting on airplanes, in a hotel room, in a conference, talking to them, bouncing ideas off them was exponentially more valuable than any passing of each other in the hallways, poking my head into their bedrooms at home. Five minutes talking on a plane about life and their goals for the future was worth an hour of our routine time at home.

Just as Zig Ziglar said there was no elevator to business success, there's also no elevator to a terrific relationship—no matter who it's with. You have to take things a step at a time. So often as a parent, when it comes to your interactions with your children, you want to go straight to the top. I understand how life gets in the way and makes it feel like you don't have time to take those steps. But what if you tried to merge your business life with your home life?

Your kids go to school? So did mine. I went to the principal and told him what I wanted to do, to get his permission and to ensure my kids wouldn't be penalized. They came up with a program that required the kids to get every teacher to sign off that they were at or exceeding the work level for that particular class, as well as to get the homework in advance, which was due when they returned.

The school agreed, and it's worked out beautifully. I have relationships with them that exceed what I once dreamed of.

I also wanted to scale my relationship with Kevin.

We're partners, and we were doing fine. We liked each other—but I knew more and better was possible. So, as I mentioned earlier, I moved my family down to Saint Petersburg for the winter so I could be in proximity to him and invest more in his mentorship of me. I spent more time with him, traveled with him, went with him nearly every place he went. I walked up the stairs to the relationship we have today, where he's not just my mentor, but my friend and partner. We gave each other permission to know, like, and trust each other.

He met me on the stairs.

BABSON COMES CALLING

You may or not be familiar with Babson College.

If you aren't, Babson College was established as a private business school back in 1919 in Wellesley, Massachusetts. It was founded by Roger Babson, and its current central focus is on entrepreneurial education. In fact, as of the writing of this book, it has been ranked as number one in that category by the Princeton Review, *Entrepreneur* magazine, and *U.S. News & World Report*. Its MBA program has also been ranked number two *globally* for career progress by *Financial Times* in 2019, with more than 41,000 alumni in 119 countries.

That is to say that this institution knows entrepreneurship.

Because of Kevin's incredible success, Babson approached him about taking his rise as one of the greatest entrepreneurs the business world had ever seen and turning it into a case study for their students. Kevin, a natural mentor and educator, quickly agreed, excited about the opportunity to pass on the same knowledge to young entrepreneurs that he had to me.

What no one could have expected—least of all Kevin—is that he'd experience his biggest failure right in the middle of it all.

CHAPTER TEN

TO BABSON AND BACK AGAIN

"I was approached by Professor Neil Churchill about this case study," Kevin told me. "I asked what all would be entailed in this. He pitched as it an opportunity to give back to the entrepreneurial community. They would send students and faculty to my business, all with signed non-disclosure agreements, and they'd observe and interview me and the other people who worked with me.

"I gave them full access. I wanted them to see both the ups and the downs of the business, because it would be insincere to say everything was all good, all the time. Having said that, the focus was primarily on how I got to where I was—what I called the rise.

"What we never saw coming is that they would also bear witness to my fall. Remember when I told you a little bit about the issue with my infomercial company?"

"Wait a minute," I said, incredulous. "You mean that happened in the middle of this case study?"

"Right in the middle of this case study," Kevin said.

"I have to hear this," I said.

BACK TO THE BEGINNING

"I started Quantum Marketing International, Inc.—or QMI—on August 27, 1988, with my brother, Tim, and with seventy-five thousand dollars in cash. We had been looking at a vacant office space down the road from my old company, Franchise America. The space had been leased by a company that had just gone bankrupt. I mean there were still plants sitting around and pictures on the wall, it was that recent. So on a Friday morning, I resigned at Franchise America and signed a lease for the office space that afternoon.

"Monday morning, we were in business—except I didn't have one dime of income lined up. I had no products, no plans—nothing. But I had to get out of Franchise America. Everyone else there wanted to come with me, but I only took my brother. I wanted a clean start to do things in the industry the way I knew they should be done. Luckily, I found Arnold Morris at a trade show, and we know what happened there."

"This is where your rise started," I said.

"Yeah, but even there we had some early problems in manufacturing. There were labor issues and even a strike. They ended up moving production facilities, which put them months behind in delivering to us. We had to hire a bunch of temps to handle all the customer service complaints. We had to go from charging the customers' cards when they ordered to waiting until the knives were shipped. We had some people so angry they called the Better Business Bureau, and even their attorney generals.

"Later, I discovered the hand-hammered wok. It was a great product, but we had an operating loss of almost a hundred thousand dollars on them due to similar production and manufacturing complications. That, along with the rapid growth we were experiencing as a company, made us continually short on cash, even though we were getting lots of orders and payments from customers.

"By January of 1989, we had grown to nine people, including an accountant and a receptionist, and even more temps in customer service. We were cruising, already making millions. But with that growth came some management problems. Part of that problem was me."

"You?" I said. "How so?"

"When I first started all of this, I had my hands in everything. I produced and edited the shows, read the scripts, sourced the products, went to the trade shows, and bought the media. As we grew, everyone in the business—and I mean everyone—still reported to me. Nobody would order merchandise without me giving the okay. By mid-1989, by the time we got to forty-five people, it was driving me crazy. If I went out of town for three days, I'd get a hundred phone calls while I was gone. If I wanted to stay small and live a short life, I could have kept on that way—but I didn't want either of those things. I brought in management for different roles, and we had our ups and downs there, but we continued to work toward scale and growth.

"Still, it was good for Babson to see and learn about these things for the case study, because elements of this led up to the fall that was on the horizon."

THE CONTINUITY CLUB

"I had formed a division of QMI called Quantum Direct," Kevin continued. "It rented the lists of all of our QMI customers and did direct mailings to advertise our television products and did outbound telemarketing. We sold the people who bought records and tapes *more* records and tapes, or the people who brought kitchen items *more* kitchen items.

"The other thing we had was called The Continuity Club, which was essentially a 'Gadget of the Month' club. It was sort of like the Columbia House deal with compact discs. People would sign up to receive a current product, and every other month after, they'd receive a card describing which product was coming next. If they didn't send the card back saying 'no,' we shipped them the item. If they liked it, they kept it, and if they didn't, they could send it back. By 1990, The Continuity Club had a total of eighty thousand members who paid a forty-dollar fee. The majority of Quantum Direct's sales were to club members."

"This sounds like trouble," I said.

"What happened was that club members were canceling and were still getting shipped the merchandise," Kevin said. "The fulfillment center was not being run properly and was giving us bad information. We had sold eighty thousand members, but eighty-two percent of them had canceled; and most of them were still getting shipments—some their initial product *twice*."

My jaw dropped. "Eighty-two percent?"

"Not only that," Kevin continued, "but these customers were mad not only because they didn't want to be members anymore, but because they were getting one, sometimes two things they didn't even ask for, and they wanted their forty dollars back. It was a huge mess.

"With the high rate of charge-backs, the credit-card processing company we were working with took three hundred thousand dollars of good charges to protect themselves from any future charge-backs. Then the bank notified us, QMI, that we were in default on our loan and that they wanted—demanded—that we pay our balance of one and a half million dollars *immediately*. Not only that, but they froze our bank account, which had about nine hundred thousand dollars in it."

THE FALL

"We were refunding every nickel that was coming in the door from our television products from QMI. Looking back, if we had never started Quantum Direct, we would have never had an issue, because QMI was profitable from the start. We had to file Chapter 11, or we would have been completely devastated and out of business completely. All of our contracts, everything we were working on *literally* stopped overnight. No one wanted to sign any business deals with a company going into bankruptcy. Why would they?"

"And all this occurred while Babson was performing the case study?" I said.

"Yep," Kevin said. "But as we've said before, from failure to phoenix, right? This whole thing turned out to be a blessing in disguise for both me and Babson."

I smiled. "Because they got to see the rise."

Kevin smiled back. "That's right. The rise, the fall, and then the rise again."

When he had taught me the principle of failure to phoenix, he had recounted how he achieved his remarkable turnaround. He sold QMI's assets to a publicly traded company on the New York Stock Exchange, becoming the second largest shareholder of this public company. They then gave stock to people he owed money in lieu of cash, taking the company's stock from less than $2 per share to $20. Even though I'd heard it once before, I still got chills. That story never gets old.

And Babson is proof positive of that.

The First Class

"The first time I got to see the case study taught," Kevin said, "was sometime in either '91 or '92. They invited me up for the last day. They had taught the students all about my initial rise to success, and the day I visited, they were on the last day of the fall. The students had no idea that there was a subsequent rise, and the faculty was going to disclose it to them at the end of the case study with me there in the audience.

"So I'm sitting in the back of this class as the professor is lecturing, and while no one there knows who I am or that I'm even there, I'm feeling pretty good about myself. I mean, I had come out of this terrible situation in pretty good shape, right?

"Let's just say that I recognize that it's a teacher's job to teach. They had to specifically point out where the big mistakes were made. Well, this professor did his job well."

"How do you mean?" I said.

"These students were making big fun of me!"

"Stop," I said. "Really?"

"I'm sitting here in the class just looking around at these people, and I couldn't help myself—I was fuming. I'm thinking to myself, *You're just a young college kid—what would you have done in the line of fire trying to decide what to do? You've built this eighty-five-million-dollar-a-year business, you're scrambling day to day, and then everything implodes—how do you handle it?* Sitting in that class, I went from feeling like Mr. Successful Entrepreneur to feeling like the emperor with no clothes.

"But when Babson gave me the opportunity to share the story of the rise after the fall, I could see their opinions start to change—even with just the idea that I saved the company. But I still had to rebuild it, right? What good was it to have couple of million shares at a dollar a share? So what if you have a couple of million dollars? You have to build *big* value.

"National Media, the company that we were going to merge with before we filed Chapter 11, finally understood the assets I had accumulated, the exclusive contracts in Europe, Latin America, and Asia—they saw we were starting a global launch of our infomercials. We were in the right place at the right time with the right people. National Media's stock was worth one dollar, and they had twelve million shares. When I did the deal with them, they had a twelve-million-dollar market cap. Three years later, the stock was close to twenty dollars a share and they had issued another twelve million shares, now up to twenty-five million shares. We went to a five-hundred-million-dollar market cap. My take of that was approximately fifty million. Not a bad deal for an asset that many of those students might have found worthless. Without that fall, we wouldn't have the story that we do today."

And Babson knew it.

BACK TO BABSON

Babson told Kevin that most case studies in their program are used for a few years at most before they move on to new things.

As with all things Kevin Harrington, his case study was not most.

In fact, Kevin's rise, fall, and rise is so impactful, so inspiring, that it has been part of Babson's curriculum for almost *30 years*.

To commemorate this, Babson College invited Kevin back for a near-30-year celebration of the use of his momentous case study—and I got to attend it with him. Kevin got to tell the story of his rise from the ashes to another group of eager entrepreneurial students who were blown away in equal measure to those who had heard this story decades ago. It was incredible to witness. Seeing these students be impacted by a story over a quarter of a century old reaffirmed the power that this story had had for me and how it had made Kevin such an inspirational mentor.

But believe it or not, something even more impactful happened while we were there.

Babson gave a select group of students, ones who had been through Kevin's case study class, the opportunity to pitch Kevin on the spot—to get feedback from the original *Shark Tank* Shark on their ideas. What was so incredible about this—so much so that I still find myself awestruck thinking about it—is that Kevin actually volunteered to start using and backing some of their ideas.

"One of the kids had this travel app called TravelSquad," he told me afterward. "I told him that if he could show me that he could actually save me money, that I'd start running my travel through his app—and I travel *a lot*, all over the world.

"Another kid had a pretty incredible drink product. So incredible that I asked him for his contact information for samples so I could hook him up with the former CEO of one of the big drink companies.

"We probably talked to fifteen to twenty kids, and what was so incredible—what was so inspiring to me—is that these kids didn't just stand up and give me their names. Every one of them had a business. One guy stood up and said he had a digital marketing business. The other said they've got a travel business. On and on.

"It was so different from my college experience. Sure, I had a business in college—but no one else I knew did. Even my son Brian—when he was in college, I got so excited thinking about how I'd get him to run a business while he was there, and he didn't want anything to do with that. He wanted to focus on being a college student—and I got that. Heck, I didn't graduate from college. How could I say anything to him if he came home with poor grades because he was trying to run a business at the same time?

"Babson is changing the game. Kids are coming out of there with businesses, contacts, and money. They learn how to raise capital, how to market, how to do digital—they've even got manufacturing there. The campus had 3-D printers and prototyping departments. Students come there with nothing and leave with a business. It's so exciting to me that this even exists.

"My first class at the University of Cincinnati? It was called Orientation to Business. Now remember, I graduated from a small school, with two hundred kids in my graduating class. I showed up on the first day of this first course and there were *eight hundred* kids. From the top of the classroom, I looked down and saw there was television. A video recording started, and it was from the professor saying they were sorry, but they couldn't be there for the first day of class—take good notes, and I'll see you next week. That was the beginning of the end for me as college went.

"You'd never see that at Babson. They have fewer than twenty-five hundred students, and that kind of small, focused learning environment produces some serious results. It was apparent in the pitches these kids were giving. They had vision and business opportunities that they had already started. In many ways, it brought things full circle. Not just coming back after thirty years. Seeing these kids was like looking at a mirror image of my younger self. It was truly inspiring."

YOU CAN DO IT, TOO

It was incredible to see Kevin interacting with these students. It took me back to that first day in Florida with Mary by my side, sitting at his kitchen table—when I knew that Kevin was the mentor I'd always been seeking.

Even with all that he's achieved, he was open to these young entrepreneurs. Excited to hear their ideas and see them do things the way he did as he was coming into his own. I could see on their faces that in their minds, they were telling themselves that there was no way Kevin Harrington was ever going to listen to their ideas. This was a man who if they Googled his name, they would see all that he's done, and for those who have never met him, that can be an impressive and intimidating thing. Yet you could see the change in their faces as they went from fear to excitement as he actively listened and even got excited himself about their ideas.

I was reminded of a book published in 2012 by a man named Bob Goff called *Love Does*. At the end of that book, Bob gave out his actual phone number. Seven years later, people still talk to me about how he used his real phone number. Of course, if you call that number today, there's a message from Bob about some other ways you can reach him as he can't possibly field all the calls that came from a best-selling book.

What it did for Goff was humanize him for his readers and admirers. It took him from this sort of mythical, abstract idea of a person and made him a *real* person. Watching Kevin speak to these students in the classroom and interact with them during their pitches, I saw the same phenomenon occurring. They saw in him that they also had the potential to accomplish what he had accomplished. They realized that they could meet Kevin Harrington and understand that he's an entrepreneur at heart just like them.

He's had ideas, just like them. He's failed, just like them. He's recovered from failure, and he's transparent in the mistakes he made and how they ultimately laid the foundation for the massive success he's realized today.

Babson was a homecoming of sorts—an opportunity to bring things full circle for Kevin in so many ways.

He let those students, those burgeoning entrepreneurs see—just as he allowed me to see—that they could do it, too.

We hope that you come away from this book with the sense that you've found something of a mentor in Kevin—and discovered opportunities for you to be a mentor in someone else's life as well. Kevin's mentorship journey is nowhere near over.

Neither is yours.

And, as it turns out, neither was mine.

EPILOGUE

"We Have to Be Timms"

It's not easy to change course in life.

When we make mistakes, we often justify them. We tell ourselves that the mistakes come from love and the desire to do the right thing for your family.

And that might be true.

But a mistake is a mistake, and if we want to do right by ourselves and our family, we have to do better.

That is really hard—and we often don't know if we are making a difference.

Sometimes we have to wait years to know if there's a payoff. When you try to change the dynamics and relationships within your family, when you want to change the trajectory of the way your kids think and act about and toward you, it's not an overnight decision. It's not even a week-long or month-long decision.

You make this decision knowing that it could take years to see any results, not knowing what those results will be.

So often we ask ourselves as parents, "Did we get this right? Was this the right way to spend our time? Was this the right decision?" Sometimes we make these big decisions, and we never get the validation of knowing whether they were right or wrong. It can take years, decades, even a generation to find out.

Sounds like starting a company, doesn't it? You make a bet, you bust your butt for years, and maybe, just maybe, it works out.

Well, with kids and with companies, it may take a while, but you do eventually find out.

HOME, AND BACK AGAIN

Not long after the Babson experience, I received an invitation to speak at something called The Marketing Academy in Budapest, Hungary. The organization wanted me to come and talk about marketing tactics, as they have a strong desire to bring the United States style of sales and marketing to Hungary.

It's important to remember that Hungary has been independent from association with the former Soviet Union for less than 30 years, so as far as being a capitalistic, free market, entrepreneurial country, it is in its infancy. The spirit of entrepreneurialism is alive there, but in many ways, it's also scary. It still feels quite foreign to the residents, and so there is a lot about it that they fear.

One thing that has resonated as true with them, though, was how they survived over centuries of being constantly occupied by other countries. They were the ping-pong ball of Europe, if you will. As such, family is vitally important to them. It grounds them because it's how they survived— by being surrounded by tight-knit families. Now, in this new capitalistic society, Mom isn't staying home anymore. She's an entrepreneur, going to work to help provide for the family. There is a new dynamic in place.

So, off to Hungary, where I was to be the keynote speaker at the academy, talking about selling—how selling is not a bad word when it's done correctly. I talked a great deal about Zig Ziglar. Incredibly, in a room of 400 entrepreneurs, when I asked how many had heard of Zig, at least 350 hands went up. Long after Zig had passed away, he still managed to leave an impact on Hungary.

So I leaned into that, spending a lot of time talking about Zig's philosophy of selling, problem solving, and helping people get what they want.

When I was approached with this opportunity, I was glad to realize that it happened to be scheduled for the beginning of the school district's fall break. That meant I could bring my family. My two younger sons are both serving active duty in the U.S. military, but my oldest, Markus, had just completed his formal military training and had a gap of free time before his next assignment, and Cassandra and Grace were on break from school, so they were excited to go.

The last day of the conference, the organizers asked me if I would come up onstage and share some thoughts and ideas about our family—specifically about my philosophy of the interaction between family and business. Then they said:

"If you don't mind, we'd love for your kids to come up onstage so the audience can see that they're here with you, and maybe ask them a few questions."

I had already prepared some thoughts around family and had prepared the kids for the idea that they might get called up onstage, and that they might even have to field some questions. Markus had been onstage with me before, so I knew he would be fine, but Cassandra and Grace had never spoken on a stage like this and, to be candid, had not planned to, so I was unsure how this all might go down.

A Big Deal

The conference up to this point had gone extraordinarily well. The audience and the organization really embraced the family and our message. It was one of those rare experiences where you just know that you're in the right place at the right time.

As I was prepared to take the stage on that last day, the lead organizer stopped me.

"You've done such a good job here, and you're such an excellent speaker that I'm afraid if you get up there and start talking about family, then we won't have time to get your kids up there. They've heard from you all week. Let's start with your children."

"Okay, I like that idea." I walked over to my kids. "Hey, instead of coming up after me, you're going to go out first. The organizer is going to ask you a few questions, and then I'll give a speech about family."

Markus was fine with it. My daughters, as expected, not so much.

"Dad, we don't mind going up onstage," Grace said, "but we don't really want to say anything."

"Yeah," Cassandra said, "maybe Markus can just speak for us."

"Right," Grace said. "We can just wave and say thank you for hosting us or something like that."

Not wanting to force anything, I agreed. They took their seats on stage, and Attila, the conference organizer, spoke.

"We've really enjoyed spending time with you. It's been really amazing. We've gotten to know your father well over the last few days. He's taught us so much about what he's learned from Zig Ziglar and Kevin Harrington. So, let me ask you, what has it been like to be the child of an entrepreneur who has learned all of these things from these incredible mentors?"

GETTING IT RIGHT

Markus answered first.

"I've learned so much working and traveling with my dad. The fact that he's an entrepreneur has given me the opportunity to see and experience things that have changed the trajectory of my life."

He stopped and looked down at his feet.

"But it wasn't always like this. My dad used to be gone all the time. He traveled so much, I barely saw him. I felt like I didn't really know him. And that was hard. But once he figured out that he wasn't giving his family what he was giving to his businesses, everything changed. He started getting it right—and his getting it right changed my life.

"Before he got it right, the last thing I ever wanted to be was an entrepreneur. I didn't want anything to do with that way of life. Now we have a relationship that's stronger than it ever was, and I'm an entrepreneur myself, because he's shown me how I can do it the right way."

I was floored.

Then Grace took the microphone. She cleared her throat and mine tightened up.

"I'm not nearly as good a speaker as Markus," she said, voice shaking, "and I'm really nervous. I don't have any fancy stories, so I'm just going to share from my heart. It was really, really hard being the child of the entrepreneur my father was. But the one he is now, he has made such a difference in my life. I've done things I never thought I could do because of my dad."

As she went on about the projects with the shoes and the surgery for the child in Africa, I looked out into the audience. It appeared as though there wasn't one person who wasn't crying—me included.

Grace then handed the microphone to Cassandra, the same Cassandra who was determined not to speak just a few minutes ago.

"I left public school to begin traveling for a year with my father, which was an incredible experience." She looked offstage to me, then back to the audience. "But before that, I didn't have a great relationship with my dad."

Her words hit me like a shot to the gut.

I'd always known this to be true—that I had only given my family a fraction of me for the sake of my businesses. That my relationships with my wife and children were suffering in the name of success. It was why I stopped on my driveway, that day years ago. But to hear those words out loud almost took my legs out from under me.

What kept me standing is what she said next.

"But when he realized that his business life and home life didn't have to be separate—that they couldn't be— that was when we developed a true love and respect for one another. That couldn't have happened if he wasn't an entrepreneur. He just had to become the right *kind* of entrepreneur. I'm so grateful that he did, and even more grateful to call him Dad, 'cause he is kind of cool."

When they came off that stage, I hugged them all tighter than I ever had before. *I* was the one who was grateful—for them, and that I had made the right choice all those years ago sitting at the end of my driveway.

That moment in Hungary was, without a doubt, one of the highlights of my entire life.

NOT ALL TIMMS

You've followed along with me on this journey, so I want to take the opportunity to be completely transparent.

Though she gave an impassioned speech about what it meant and what she learned about being the child of an entrepreneur, Cassandra is not my biological daughter.

My wife, Ann, and I have a blended family. I have two daughters and one son. Ann has two sons and one daughter. We are the modern-day Brady Bunch.

I wanted to share this with you because I know that there are so many of you entrepreneurs out there who are struggling to bring your families together.

Some of you might be divorced, or have been impacted by divorce in some way, or your children have.

Creating this "business of family" created the common ground for our two families to blend. Instead of inhabiting the same space, we became a unit.

We mistakenly thought in the beginning that because we both had custody of our children from our previous marriages that everything would be just fine. They'd be brothers and sisters, and everything would be great.

It wasn't. Everything was his and hers, theirs and ours. It can be exceedingly difficult to blend a family—particularly siblings. They need some common ground from which to draw to be a unified front.

Remember that we decided to incorporate our family. We did that quite literally. The name of our company is

2BTimms. At the time that we decided to do this, Cassandra, along with Kavyn and Zachary, Ann's two boys, did not have my last name. When we announced the family business and we started to have shareholder meetings, Cassandra spoke up.

"If we're going to be shareholders in the family business, then we have an issue here," she said.

"What is it?" I said.

"We don't have the right last name. If it's 2BTimms, then we need to be Timms."

The moment brought tears to my eyes. With that, our children asked to have their names changed to Timm. Mind you, they were older at this point, all teenagers.

What is still so overwhelming to me is that it wasn't the fact that I married their mom that made them want to change their last name. It was the fact that they now had a common ground—a common language to speak, such that they could relate to one another and truly feel like family.

We were—and are—all part of the family business.

What about You?

It is my and Kevin's sincere hope that this book has helped you find your driveway moment—that in this book you discovered some ways not only to improve your entrepreneurial ventures and scale your business, but to scale your relationships.

We invite you to share with us how you have struggled with merging your business and family. E-mail us at story@mentortomillionsbook.com and tell us your story.

We look forward to hearing from you soon.

FREE RESOURCES FOR YOUR SUCCESS

10 Steps to a Perfect Pitch
Kevin Harrington

Become a pitch master and craft your perfect pitch in just a few minutes. You'll learn Kevin's PROVEN PROCESS that has rocketed 20+ businesses to over $100 million in revenue each and created thousands of first-time millionaires!
www.kevinharrington.tv/perfectpitch

Key Person of Influence Roadmap
Kevin Harrington

This is a complete roadmap where you'll discover the 7-step system for becoming a highly valued, sought-after expert in your industry and use this platform to prime your business for exponential growth.
www.kevinharrington.tv/kpi

Sharkpreneur Podcast
Kevin Harrington

The Sharkpreneur Podcast features Kevin Harrington, Seth Greene, and some of today's top business leaders sharing straight talk about what it takes to explode your business.
www.kevinharrington.tv/podcast

You Can Win at Home
Like You Win at Work
Mark Timm

Business leaders can experience great success at work, but feel totally lost when it comes to kids and family. But it doesn't have to be this way. What if you ran your family like you ran your business? The fact is business leaders already know more than they think they do about how to be a confident parent. This book shares five proven strategies to win at home like you win at work.
www.marktimm.com/win

Essential Steps to
Productive Family Meetings
Mark Timm

Family Meeting Guide will help you get started and overcome common mistakes parents make when trying to conduct productive family meetings.
www.marktimm.com/familymeeting

Family CEO Podcast
Mark Timm

The Family CEO podcast features Mark Timm and some of today's most successful entrepreneurs who are not only successful business gurus but also put high importance on leading their families. This podcast is all about equipping you with proven techniques to lead your family with confidence and clarity as well as thrive in your business. You already have ALL you need to have to lead your family to success and long-lasting legacy.
www.marktimm.com/podcast

BUT WAIT,
THERE'S MORE!

Hello, readers! Kevin Harrington here.

Unless you've been living under a rock for the last 30 years or so, you've seen your share of infomercials. In fact, I'm willing to bet there are a few items in your home you might have purchased from one—maybe even one I put together.

Remember the feeling you got as you watched? How every little detail got you closer and closer to pulling that credit card out of your wallet or purse? Then just as you were ready to dial that toll-free number, the announcer, as if he knew you had the telephone in your hand, shouts at you through the screen:

"But wait—there's more!"

And you did wait. Even though you were about to order, you still had a little hesitation. You asked yourself if you really did want to make those promised four easy payments. Then they hit you with the clincher—the added bonus that made the sale a foregone conclusion.

We refer to that as *value stacking*. Think of the concept like this: transactional selling or pitching is like a scale. Price sits on one side of the scale, while the features and benefits of the product offered rest on the other. A consumer will only buy that product when the scale tips in their favor—when they're getting more value than the price they're paying.

Oftentimes in the infomercial world, the seller created a scenario where the consumer could see the value in their purchase, but the scales were practically even. They were on the precipice of buying, but they needed a reason to dial that number.

"But wait—there's more!" is what pushed them over the edge—where consumers said, "I'm in," and committed to the product. By telling customers, "Don't buy yet, because what I'm about to offer you is worth as much as everything else I've offered to this point," the salespeople left them with what they saw as a truly irresistible offer.

It took them to that psychological place so frequently and so successfully that virtually every television marketer took up the strategy, because it essentially meant they could scale to a hundred-million-dollar product. In fact, the practice became so successful that the phrase became a part of our cultural lexicon.

So why am I telling you this?

Because I realize that even if you enjoyed this book and saw the value in the principles in it, you still might be thinking: *What does it look like to put these things in action in the real world? How can I make these principles work for me?*

Can you guess what I'm going to say?

But wait—there's more!

That's right, friends, I'm about to blow your mind with some added value that will allow you to put these strategies to work. I'm going to share with you how we used every concept in the preceding chapters to put this book in your hands.

Remember in Chapter 9 we discussed a CEO and co-founder who got out of his own way and fired himself so that his company could scale?

If you haven't guessed by now, that person was none other than Tucker Max, founder of Scribe Media.

You might ask, "What does it matter that it was Tucker Max, and why do I care about Scribe Media?"

It's simple. The principles in this book that I taught Mark Timm—and by extension, you—are what brought us to Tucker and his company. We made him and Scribe Media a part of our dream team so that we could share these concepts and ideals with you.

First, we had to *get the right mind-set* about writing a book. We vividly imagined, ardently desired, sincerely believed, and enthusiastically acted upon our desire to create a book for our fellow entrepreneurs, so we knew that it must inevitably come to pass. However, we knew that neither of us knew how to write a book, but we couldn't let our fear keep us from acting.

So we had *to engage our aggressive curiosity.* That came in the form of asking anyone we encountered, but particularly people we knew and trusted, "Who do you know who can help us write a book?" Fortunately for us, it didn't take long before we were put on the path toward Scribe Media.

Then we had to *get focused and make a plan.* Just because we found the company that could help us accomplish this goal didn't mean it wouldn't still require planning on our part. There were time commitments that had to be made. Schedules to accommodate and rearrange. However, we couldn't plan it to death. Once we figured it out 80 percent of the way, there was only one thing to do next.

That was to *take action*—and that was about as simple as it gets. The time for talking about writing this book was done. It was now time to do it.

While we engaged in the process, there were occasions when we had to *go from failure to phoenix.* We'd discover certain stories weren't landing as we intended, or that they weren't relevant at all to the lesson we were attempting to share. Stepping back, reframing, and learning from what didn't work only made the process more efficient as we went on.

Working with Tucker and his team was the ultimate example of *multiplying our efforts.* We achieved the exponential result of putting this book in your hands because we made sure to focus on *who* would help us to write this book, *not how* we were going to get it done.

As a result of this successful endeavor, Tucker and Scribe Media, as we mentioned, are now an integral part of our dream team. When we decide to write more books— and we will—Scribe Media will be our go-to for those projects. We could not have done this without them.

In the end, the only way to *get scale* in writing this book was for us to realize we needed to get out of our own way and let someone else take the wheel. Mark and I could not be happier with the end product—and we hope you are, too.

But it's not enough for us to hope that you're satisfied with the book. We want you to walk away feeling that you got more value than you paid for.

The fact that this book is in your hands is proof that these principles work. What if you were put on this earth to impact millions, and the only thing keeping you from doing so is needing the ability to say what's trapped inside your head and heart? We know that as fellow entrepreneurs you have a story to tell. And while we all might have stories to tell, we're not all storytellers. That shouldn't keep you from sharing what you know with the world.

It is the mission of Tucker and his team at Scribe Media to "Unlock the World's Wisdom," and Mark and I want to hand you the key. We invite you to meet them at www.mentortomillionsbook.com/scribe. We look forward to seeing your book in the world as the first step on your path to mentor others.

Thank you for taking this journey with us. We hope to meet you somewhere on yours.

INDEX

A

Ab Isolator, 92–94, 133
action, 69–83
  acting on ideas ("feeding the right fire"), 69–73
  acting quickly for, 75–77
  Business Model Generation (Osterwalder) on, 57–58
  GoFundMe example of, 80–83
  mind-set for, 19–21
  overinvestment and, 73–75
  as principle *in action*, 166
  success vs. confidence for, 78–80
aggressive curiosity, 37–51
  flipping paradigms with, 48–50
  innovating with, 38–39, 42–47
  as principle in action, 165–166
  for researching trends, 39–42, 47–48
  time management and margin, 37–38, 50–51
Amazon, 129, 134
Arab Radio and Television Network (ART, Saudi Arabia), 78–80
The Art of the Deal (Trump and Schwartz), 75–76
Ask Live with Ryan Levesque, 96–97

B

Babee Tenda, 9–11
Babson, Roger, 141

Babson College, 143–153
  entrepreneurship focus of, 141
  history of, 140–141
  QMI case study, class, 148–153
  QMI case study, events, 143–148
Balter, Neil, 15
Bannister, Roger, 26
Blockbuster Video, 132
blue ocean marketing channels, 128–131
budget, hiring and, 113, 117–119
Buffett, Warren, 48
Business Model Generation (Osterwalder), 57–58
business plans. *see also* focus and planning
  five-year vs. six-month, 55–56, 60
    nine steps to, 56–59
  butterfly metaphor, 94

C

California Closets, 15
canvas business modeling, 59–61, 65–68
carbon fiber eyeglass cleaner, 129–131
Celsius, 134–136
Chubby Checker Twist-A-Sizer, 87–89
Churchill, Neil, 143
Claure, Marcelo, 104

closing techniques, 45–46

competition, blue ocean marketing channels vs., 128–131

confidence, success vs., 78–80

The Continuity Club, 146

Cottage Garden, 64

Cuban, Mark, 3

curiosity. *see* aggressive curiosity

customers, *Business Model Generation* (Osterwalder) on, 57–58. *see also* sales techniques; scaling of business

D

Discovery Channel, 44

DISC personality profile, xiii–xiv, 123

distribution channels, *Business Model Generation* (Osterwalder) on, 57–58

dream team, 127–141
    of executives, 124–125
    families as, 122–124
    flipping paradigms with team, 48–50
    hiring and finances, 113, 117–119
    resisting compromise for, 113–116
    sharing profit with, 114, 120–122

E

efforts, multiplying. *see* multiplying efforts

Entrepreneur Franchising Center, 43

Entrepreneur (magazine), 43

entrepreneurship. *see also* aggressive curiosity; Babson College; mind-set
    bootstrapping vs. dream teams for, 119
    failure experienced by entrepreneurs, 88

five-year vs. six-month business plans for, 55–56, 60

EO (Entrepreneur's Organization), 17

Essential Steps to Productive Family Meetings (Timm), 164

exponential growth. *see* multiplying efforts

F

Facebook, 130–131

failure to phoenix, 85–98
    Ab Isolator example of, 92–94
    children learning from, 94–98
    failing fast and moving on, 85–87
    learning from, 89–92
    overcoming, with action, 70
    overcoming fear of, 24–25
    as principle in action, 166
    Quantum Marketing International, Inc. (QMI) case study, 143–153
    rising like phoenix from, 24, 86, 94–95, 147, 166
    Twist-A-Sizer example of, 87–89
    vivid imagination for, 23–24

fair dealing, 21–22

families. *see also individual Timm family members*
    action and, 80–83
    allowing children to learn from failure, 94–98
    as businesses, xi–xx, 155–162
    curiosity and focus for family meetings, 50–51
    as dream team, 122–124
    mind-set for family meetings, 28–29, 33–34
    planning and, 65–68
    resources for, 164
    scaling relationships with, 137–140

fear, overcoming, 24–25

"feeding the right fire" (acting on ideas), 69–73

Fifth Third Bank (Cincinnati), 4
fishbone model for problem solving, 59
fishing in other ponds (looking outside your ecosystem), 106–109
focus and planning, 53–68
    canvas business modeling for, 59–61, 65–68
    duplicating success with, 61–65
    family meetings and, 50–51
    fishbone model for problem solving, 59
    five-year vs. six-month business plans, 55–56, 60
    mind-set and belief for, 26
    nine steps to business planning, 56–59
    overcoming perfectionism for, 53, 54
    as principle in action, 166
    seventy-five or eighty percent level plan for, 54–56
    spending and elaborate planning problem, 69–73
Franchise America (business name), 15–17, 42–46, 144
Franchise America (television show), 45
franchising
    Harrington's early experience with, 15–16
    scaling with, 132

G

Gannett, 60
Gates, Bill, 48
Gazelle, 93–94
Ginsu knives, 22–23, 101–102, 114–115, 144
Goff, Bob, 152–153
GoFundMe, 80–83
growth, exponential. *see* multiplying efforts

growth, linear, 127, 131–132
Guardian, 12–13

H

Harrington, Brian, 21, 39, 151
Harrington, Kevin, 1–17. *see also* action; aggressive curiosity; dream team; failure to phoenix; focus and planning; infomercials; mind-set; multiplying efforts; Quantum Marketing International, Inc. (QMI) case study
    biographical information and early businesses, 4–15, 151
    contact information, 162
    father of, 20, 89–90
    Franchise America, 15–17, 42–46, 144
    Ginsu knives business of, 22–23, 101–102, 114–115, 144
    mentoring by, 1–4, 16–17
    mind-set of, 15–17, 19–21
    Own Your Own Business (television show), 45
    resources, 163
    small events held by, 129–131
    StarShop, 103–104
Harrington Enterprises, 16
Harrington's Irish Pub, 6
hiring. *see* dream team
holograms, 38–39
HSN, 130

I

infomercials
    birth of, 44–46, 100
    Ginsu knives, 22–23, 101–102, 114–115, 144
    Harrington's start in, 42–46
    success of, 136–137
    Trump and, 77
innovating, with aggressive curiosity, 38–39, 42–47

K

Kamel, Saleh, 78–80
Kellogg's, 60
Key Person of Influence Roadmap (Harrington), 163
Kispert, Louis, 4

L

Levesque, Ryan, 96–97
linear growth vs. scaling, 127, 131–132
Little, Tony, 92–94, 133
looking outside your ecosystem (fishing in other ponds), 106–109
L'Oréal, 117–118
Love Does (Goff), 152–153

M

margin, time as, 37–38, 50–51
The Marketing Academy (Budapest, Hungary), 157–162
Markus (frame and décor line), 71–73
Mary's Moments, 71–73
masterminds, 70
Max, Tucker, 165–166
mentorship. *see also* Ziglar, Zig
    Harrington and, 1–4, 16–17
    importance of, xv–xx
    mind-set and, 34–35
Meyer, Paul J., 23
mind-set, 19–35
    for exponential thinking, 22–23, 108
    for fair dealing, 21–22
    for flipping paradigms, 48–50
    of Harrington, 15–17, 19–21
    mentorship and, 34–35
    motivation and, 27–31
    overcoming fear with, 24–25
    overcoming procrastinating perfectionism with, 25–27
    as principle in action, 165

for vivid imagination, 23–24, 32–34
Morris, Arnold, 101–102, 106–107, 114–115, 144
motivation
    Business Model Generation (Osterwalder) on, 57–58
    mind-set and, 27–31
multiplying efforts, 99–111
    exponential thinking for, 22–23, 99–101, 108
    Ginsu knives example, 22–23, 101–102, 114–115, 144
    looking outside your ecosystem (fishing in other ponds) for, 106–109
    as principle in action, 166
    transformational relationships for, 105–106
    trust and, 108–109, 111
    who vs. how, 102–104, 109–111
    win-win relationships for, 3, 21, 105–106, 111, 119

N

National Media, 149
Netflix, 132

O

Orbit, 79–80
Osterwalder, Alexander, 57–58
outbound marketing, *Franchise America* (television show) as, 45. *see also* infomercials
overinvestment, danger of, 73–75
ownership, dream team and, 114, 120–122
Own Your Own Business (television show), 45
OxiClean, 46

P

paradigms, flipping, 48–50
perfectionism, procrastinating and, 25–27, 53, 54

phoenix. *see* failure to phoenix

planning. *see* focus and planning

pricing psychology, 132–134

Proactiv, 46

problem solving
canvas business modeling for, 59–61, 65–68
fishbone model for, 59

Product Launch Formula, 96

product trends, researching, 39–42, 47–48

Q

Quantum Marketing International, Inc. (QMI) case study
class taught about, 148–153
events, 143–148

QVC, 130

R

research, curiosity and, 39–42, 47–48

resources, *Business Model Generation* (Osterwalder) on, 57–58

Rida, Flo, 135

S

sales techniques
advertising and call to action, 46
Business Model Generation (Osterwalder) on, 57–58
clearancing, 63
closing, 45–46
isolating the objection, 11

Saudi Arabia, Arab Radio and Television Network in, 78–80

scaling of business, 127–141. *see also* Babson College; focus and planning; multiplying efforts
blue ocean marketing channels for, 128–131
Celsius example of, 134–136
getting out of your own way for, 128, 165-166

Harrington's early experience with, 9

linear growth vs. scaling, 127, 131–132

mind-set for, 21–22, 29–31

pricing psychology and, 132–134

as principle in action, 166

scaling of relationships and, 137–141

WHSmith example of, 136–137

Schwartz, Tony, 75–76

Scribe Media, 165–166

Secrets of Closing the Sale (Ziglar), 45–46

See You at the Top (Ziglar), 16

Shark Tank (television show), 2–3, 121

Shoes for Change, 67–68, 109–110, 161

Small Business Center, 16

software as a service (SaaS), 133–134

Sprint, 104

StarShop, 103–104

StrengthsFinder test, 123

success, confidence vs., 78–80

sugar glider business, 110–111

Sullivan, Dan, 102

Sutton, Tom, 89

SWOT (strengths, weaknesses, opportunities, threats) analysis, 56

T

team. *see* dream team

10 Steps to a Perfect Pitch (Harrington), 163

time management
acting quickly, 75–77
aggressive curiosity and, 37–38, 48–51

Timm, Ann, 156

Timm, Cassandra, 29–31, 156, 157, 159–162

Timm, Grace, 65–68, 80–83,
109–110, 122–124, 138–139,
159–162
Timm, Kavyn, 157
Timm, Mark. *see also* families
contact information, 162
early businesses of, 61–64
Harrington as business partner
of, 19–21, 37–38
interviews of Harrington by,
1–4
personal assistant of, 29–31
resources, 164
Timm, Markus, 96–97, 105, 122,
158–162
Timm, Mary, xvi–xvii, 1–4, 7–8,
10–12, 14, 66, 95, 110–111
Timm, Zachary, 157
TOMS Shoes, 110
Trane, 13–14
transformational relationships,
105–106
TravelSquad, 150
trends, aggressive curiosity for,
39–42, 47–48
Tri State Heating and Cooling, 14
Trump, Donald, 75–78
trust, 108–109, 111
turtle on a fence post metaphor,
32–34
Twist-A-Sizer, 87–89
2BTimms, 157–162

U

uniqueness, xiii–xiv, 122–124

V

value, multiplying, 22–23. *see also*
multiplying efforts

vivid imagination, 23–24, 32–34
volunteering, 66–68

W

Walker, Jeff, 96
Walmart, 129
Wealth Bowl, 19–21
who vs. how, for multiplying
efforts, 102–104, 109–111
WHSmith, 136–137
win-win relationships, 3, 21, 105–
106, 111, 119. *see also*
multiplying efforts

X

Xponential, Inc., 90–92

Y

You Can Win at Home Like You
Win at Work (Timm), 164

Z

Ziglar, Tom, 60
Ziglar, Zig
See You at the Top, 16
on action, 78
on Bannister's example, 26
legacy of, 3–4, 38–39, 73–75,
158
mentorship by, xv
mind-set and, 32
planning and, 54
Secrets of Closing the Sale, 45–46
on success, 91

ACKNOWLEDGMENTS

KEVIN HARRINGTON

I'd like to thank a few special people who made this book possible.

I want to start by acknowledging the most important people in my life: my family.

My mother, Mary, and my wife, Crystal, who both helped guide me through and deal with the ups and downs of being an entrepreneur.

My two kids, Brian and Nicholas, of course—they are both a source of inspiration and a reason for me to work so hard.

And my grandkids, who all keep me motivated every day to keep going and to push our legacy forward.

Now I'd like to thank the team behind the book.

First, I'd like to thank Tucker Max and his team at Scribe Media. Scribe enabled me to pour my entire life out and ensure it was organized in a way that would help teach the world. Their approach to this entire process has brought out more stories of mine that I forgot about over the years. Tucker has personally shaped this book and my part of it to be the best it can be, not only for me, but for everyone.

Second, I'd like to thank John Vercher, also from Scribe. Tucker was part of the vision for this book, but John did the actual work of making the idea work on the page, and for that, he deserves immense credit. If this book reads well, it's because of John.

Third, Reid Tracy, the owner of Hay House, and Anne Barthel, our editor, and the rest of the amazing team. Hay House has been absolutely incredible to work with. Everyone has been top notch. Reid Tracy is a visionary who took a chance on a book idea that was very different from the conventional business book. The publishing industry, just like every other industry, is changing. I see Reid leading the way, and am proud to be part of this.

I also want to acknowledge all of my business partners, vendors, service providers, and everyone around me who works with me in any capacity. I won't name them all here, but if you work with me in any capacity—whether as a partner, investor, service provider, or anything in between—thank you. I appreciate you. It's not possible to do this alone, and I value you very much. Entrepreneurship is a battle where you need a solid team with you, so thank you to everyone who I have worked with, past, present, and future!

We also want to thank our friend Eric "ERock" Christopher, who helped with many things, including coming up with the name.

Last, but far from least, I need to mention my co-author, Mark Timm.

The journey that we've both been on since meeting each other has been nothing short of phenomenal. We've spent countless hours together, traveling, golfing, talking, connecting, and of course—starting businesses together. That time is what made this book what it is. Even though

I've worked with family for my whole life, the perspective he gave me about business and family was a complete game changer. Even though I mentored Mark, he probably helped me at least as much as I've helped him—especially in terms of family—and for that, I will be forever grateful.

MARK TIMM

It is impossible to thank everyone who has had an impact on making this book a reality, but there are a few who deserve specific mention here.

First, as a man of faith I give all the credit for who I am and ever hope to be to God the creator and giver of all things. Thank you for blessing me with such amazing people in my life!

My wife, Ann, for supporting me through this entire book writing process. From the moment Kevin and I committed to this book, I am sure she did not know it would mean that she was going to be my audience of one as I fleshed out every chapter and every concept of the book with her before it made it onto paper. Thank you for your patience, for listening, for your much-needed input and for just smiling at me when I finished a long-winded passionate diatribe for one of the chapter concepts. Sometimes that smile was all I needed to fuel up my tank for the next chapter.

My six children, Markus, Kavyn, Zachary, Mary, Cassandra, and Grace. Being your dad is the greatest joy and accomplishment of my life. Thank you for all of our many adventures and life lessons that you taught me and you allowed me to teach you. And most of all thank you for letting me share many of those in this book for the hope that others can learn and benefit from them. I'm so proud of each one of you.

My parents, Larry and Ruth Timm, and my brother, Ron, and sister, Becky, thank you for always being there for me. My parents deserve a lot of the credit for this book, as they have made so many sacrifices for me throughout my life and set so many examples for me to follow. The work ethic and values they instilled in me at a young age are largely what makes me the man I am today and gives me the intense desire to share with my own family and to as many others as will listen.

My first mentors, Grandpa Charlie, Grandpa Bob, and Grandpa Wade. I was so incredibly blessed to have all three of these strong, God-loving men in my life throughout my entire youth. They taught me to love, to live, and to lead. I am forever grateful for each of these men and plan to spend the rest of my life living up to the legacy they left behind.

The children of Zig Ziglar deserve special acknowledgement. Thank you, Tom, Julie, and Cindy, for trusting me enough to introduce me to Kevin Harrington. I truly value our friendship and the faith that each of you have. I can't help but smile every time I think of each of you and know that your father is smiling down from Heaven on each one of you. You are his living legacy!

Tucker Max for taking the time to really listen to the stories that Kevin and I were sharing and for landing on the concept of this book. *Mentor to Millions* would not have happened without your vision and direction. And your constant reminder that the only thing that matters if you want to have a successful book is to first, "just write a [darn] good book." Though you may have said it with slightly more colorful language!

Reid Tracy and the entire Hay House team. Reid, you and your team took a chance on Kevin and me and provided the catalyst and commitment for us to deliver a manuscript that would be worthy of Hay House. Thank you for that belief in us and for your friendship.

John Vercher, thank you for the many many hours we spent together on this book. I remember thinking after week one of what would become 12 weeks of writing for this book that this was going to be hard to complete. But your constant encouragement and your ability to elevate ideas and narratives was truly a thing of beauty. The weeks flew by and we are all so proud of the final manuscript.

Brian, Izabela, Chris, Ronda, Tifny, Lori, Melanie. You all represented the "TEAM" who worked tirelessly behind the scenes to support, critique, and inspire this book to become a reality. Kevin and I can't thank you enough for your effort and encouragement.

My mentor and co-author of this book, Kevin Harrington. I saved Kevin for last, because it's hard to overstate his impact. I still remember our first conversation and my first visit to your home. In both of those I had one of my kiddos by my side. You immediately embraced them being with me and were so kind to them and so encouraging of them. That kindness and embrace set the stage for me to desire to become your best student as you provided me mentorship and wisdom. Thank you for all of the many adventures and the hours of conversations that framed our relationship. I want to also thank your wife, Crystal, for sharing her husband, and your sons, Brian and Nick, for sharing their father with me over the past few years.

And lastly, to all of the entrepreneurs, business leaders, and readers of this book who desire to have mentors and to be mentors to others, I thank you! It will be you that changes the world one mentor at a time!

ABOUT THE
AUTHORS

As an original "shark" on the hit TV show *Shark Tank*, the creator of the infomercial, pioneer of the As Seen on TV brand, and co-founding board member of the Entrepreneur's Organization, **Kevin Harrington** has pushed past all the questions and excuses to repeatedly enjoy 100X success. His legendary work behind the scenes of business ventures has produced well over $5 billion in global sales, the launch of more than 500 products, and the making of dozens of millionaires. He's launched massively successful products like The Food Saver, Ginsu Knives, The Great Wok of China, The Flying Lure, and many more. He has worked with amazing celebrities like Billie Mays, Tony Little, Jack LaLanne, and George Foreman, to name a few. Kevin's been called the Entrepreneur's Entrepreneur and the Entrepreneur Answer Man, because he knows the challenges unique to start-ups and has a special passion for helping entrepreneurs succeed. Website: kevinharrington.tv.

Mark Timm has been a serial entrepreneur and exponential-thinking practitioner for two decades. He has started more than a dozen companies, several of which have multiplied and been sold. He has spoken professionally for more than 25 years, giving thousands of speeches to over a million people around the globe. Mark's greatest value comes from being a master collaborator who brings people together to accomplish far more than anyone imagined. His strategic vision enables him to see future possibilities and strategically position assets and systems to take full advantage of what's next. Today, Mark believes his most important role is CEO of the most valuable business in the world: his family of six young adults with his wife, Ann. His own experience of dealing with entrepreneurial challenges fueled his passion for helping people balance the demands of family life and business. Website: www.marktimm.com.

We hope you enjoyed this Hay House book. If you'd like to receive our online catalog featuring additional information on Hay House books and products, or if you'd like to find out more about the Hay Foundation, please contact:

Hay House, Inc., P.O. Box 5100, Carlsbad, CA 92018-5100
(760) 431-7695 or (800) 654-5126
(760) 431-6948 (fax) or (800) 650-5115 (fax)
www.hayhouse.com® • www.hayfoundation.org

———

Published in Australia by: Hay House Australia Pty. Ltd.,
18/36 Ralph St., Alexandria NSW 2015
Phone: 612-9669-4299 • *Fax:* 612-9669-4144
www.hayhouse.com.au

Published in the United Kingdom by: Hay House UK, Ltd.,
The Sixth Floor, Watson House, 54 Baker Street, London W1U 7BU
Phone: +44 (0)20 3927 7290 • *Fax:* +44 (0)20 3927 7291
www.hayhouse.co.uk

Published in India by: Hay House Publishers India,
Muskaan Complex, Plot No. 3, B-2, Vasant Kunj, New Delhi 110 070
Phone: 91-11-4176-1620 • *Fax:* 91-11-4176-1630
www.hayhouse.co.in

———

Access New Knowledge.
Anytime. Anywhere.

Learn and evolve at your own pace
with the world's leading experts.

www.hayhouseU.com